Mathematics

Fiona McGill
Mary Nathan
Ric Pimentel

Series editors: Graham Newman
Pete Sherran

Core 8

CAMBRIDGE
UNIVERSITY PRESS

CAMBRIDGE UNIVERSITY PRESS
Cambridge, New York, Melbourne, Madrid, Cape Town, Singapore, São Paulo, Delhi

Cambridge University Press
The Edinburgh Building, Cambridge CB2 8RU, UK

www.cambridge.org
Information on this title: www.cambridge.org/9780521723800

© Cambridge University Press 2009

First published 2009

Book printed in the United Kingdom at the University Press, Cambridge

A catalogue record for this publication is available from the British Library

ISBN 978-0-521-72380-0 paperback with CD-ROM

Additional resources for this publication at essentials.cambridge.org/mathematics

Contents

Introduction		iv
N1.1	**Integers**	**1**
N1.2	**Powers and roots**	**5**
N1.3	**Multiples, factors and primes**	**9**
A1.1	Generating sequences	13
A1.2	Describing sequences	17
GM1.1	Angles	21
GM1.2	Lines, shapes and coordinates	25
GM1.3	Constructions (1)	29
S1.1	Chance and probabilty	33
S1.2	Probability	36
S1.3	Experimental probability	41
N2.1	**Fractions and decimals**	**45**
N2.2	**Calculations with fractions**	**48**
N2.3	**Percentages**	**53**
N2.4	**Mental methods (1)**	**59**
A2.1	Simplifying expressions	62
A2.2	Using equations	65
A2.3	Formulae	70
GM2.1	Area	73
GM2.2	Volume	79
GM2.3	Plans and elevations	82
GM2.4	Units of measurement	85
A3.1	Functions	88
A3.2	Functions and mappings	90
A3.3	Functions and graphs	92
N3.1	**Place value, ordering and rounding**	**96**
N3.2	**Mental methods (2)**	**100**
N3.3	**Written methods**	**105**
N3.4	**Using a calculator**	**108**
GM3.1	Congruence	112
GM3.2	Reflection, rotation and translation	114
GM3.3	Enlargement	123
S2.1	Surveys	126
S2.2	Analysing data (1)	131
S2.3	Representing data	135
S2.4	Interpreting data	141
N4.1	**Order of operations**	**145**
N4.2	**Checking**	**147**
N4.3	**Ratios**	**149**
N4.4	**Graphs of real-life situations**	**154**
A4.1	Formulae and expressions	158
A4.2	Using graphs	161
GM4.1	Scale drawing	165
GM4.2	Constructions (2)	167
GM4.3	Loci	170
GM4.4	Bearings	174
S3.1	Collecting data	178
S3.2	Analysing data (2)	181
S3.3	Comparing distributions	184

Introduction

Take advantage of the pupil CD

Cambridge Essentials Mathematics comes with a pupil CD in the back. This contains the entire book as an interactive PDF file, which you can read on your computer using free Adobe Reader software from Adobe (www.adobe.com/products/acrobat/readstep2.html). As well as the material you can see in the book, the PDF file gives you extras when you click on the buttons you will see on most pages; see the inside front cover for a brief explanation of these.

To use the CD, simply insert it into the CD or DVD drive of your computer. You will be prompted to install the contents of the CD to your hard drive. Installing will make it easier to use the PDF file, because the installer creates an icon on your desktop that launches the PDF directly. However, it will run just as well straight from the CD.

If you want to install the contents of the disc onto your hard disc yourself, this is easily done. Just open the disc contents in your file manager (for Apple Macs, double click on the CD icon on your desktop; for Windows, open My Computer and double click on your CD drive icon), select all the files and folders and copy them wherever you want.

Take advantage of the teacher CD

The *Teacher Material* CD-ROM for *Cambridge Essentials Mathematics* contains enhanced interactive PDFs. As well as all the features of the pupil PDF, teachers also have access to e-learning materials and links to the *Essentials Mathematics* Planner – a new website with a full lesson planning tool, including worksheets, homeworks, assessment materials and guidance. The e-learning materials are also fully integrated into the Planner, letting you see the animations in context and alongside all the other materials.

Integers

- Multiplying and dividing integers

Keywords

You should know

explanation 1a   explanation 1b

1 Work these out.

a $4 - 8$ b $-9 + 23$ c $26 - 32$ d $-18 + 36$

e $14 + 17 - 20$ f $-22 - 13 + 16$ g $-12 + 15 + 26$ h $-32 - 8 + 15$

2 Copy and complete these.

a $5 + -2 = 5 \square 2 = \square$ b $-3 - -7 = -3 \square 7 = \square$

c $0 - -9 = 0 \square 9 = \square$ d $-11 + -12 - -6 = -11 \square 12 \square 6 = \square$

e $20 + -13 - -15 = 20 \square 13 \square 15 = \square$

f $14 - -24 + -18 = 14 \square 24 \square 18 = \square$

3 Work these out.

a $14 - -15$ b $-21 - 12$ c $42 + -15$

d $-33 + -12$ e $-15 - -12 + 4$ f $18 - -23 + -30$

g $-22 + -4 - -8$ h $-26 - -19 + 10$ i $14 - 6 - -18$

4 Copy and complete the table.

First number	18	7	11	3	−4	−7	−12	
Second number	13	12	−2		−6		−5	−9
First number − second number	5			1		0		4

5 Copy and complete these subtraction walls. Subtract the right-hand number from the left-hand number and write the answer below the two numbers.

a

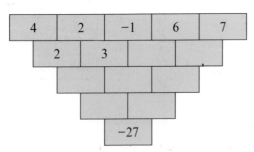

b

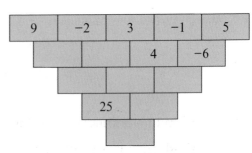

6 Lee has £56 pounds in his savings account. On Saturday he takes out £14 to buy a DVD. He receives £25 for his birthday which he pays into his account.

a How much is now in his account?

b How much more is now in his account than before he bought the DVD?

7 Use the patterns in these numbers to copy and complete these multiplication tables.

a i $3 \times 3 = 9$

$2 \times 3 = \square$

$1 \times 3 = 3$

$0 \times 3 = 0$

$-1 \times 3 = -3$

$-2 \times 3 = \square$

$-3 \times 3 = -9$

ii $3 \times -3 = -9$

$2 \times -3 = \square$

$1 \times -3 = -3$

$0 \times -3 = \square$

$-1 \times -3 = \square$

$-2 \times -3 = 6$

$-3 \times -3 = \square$

b Describe the pattern in the answer columns.

c What do you notice about the answer when a negative number and a positive number are multiplied together?

d What can you say about the answer when two negative numbers are multiplied together?

explanation 2

8 Work these out.

a 2×-6 b -7×-4 c -3×7 d 9×-8

e 5×-12 f -8×15 g -10×-23 h -6×20

i -16×-4 j -100×32 k 50×-14 l -25×-5

9 a Find two numbers such that $\square \times \square = -8$.

   b Find three more pairs of numbers that multiply to give -8.

10 Find two numbers that multiply to give these numbers.

a -10 b -6 c -14 d 55 e -21

11 Find three more different pairs of numbers that multiply to give each number in question **10**.

12 a Find two numbers that add to give 2 and multiply to give -15.

   b Find two numbers that add to give -10 and multiply to give 24.

13 Copy and complete this multiplication grid.

$\times$	-2		3	-7
		20		
-9		-45		
			-9	
				-42

explanation 3

14 Work these out.

a $45 \div -5$ b $-36 \div -4$ c $-20 \div 2$ d $-30 \div 6$

e $56 \div -7$ f $72 \div -8$ g $-60 \div 4$ h $-96 \div -12$

i $-120 \div -8$ j $64 \div -8$ k $-48 \div -3$ l $100 \div -25$

15 a How many times does -3 fit into -12?

b How many times does -7 fit into -63?

16 Using multiplication or division and positive and negative numbers, write four calculations that give each answer.

a -16 **b** 32 **c** -42 **d** -60

17 Given $-3 \times 4 = -12$, you can write three more facts:

$4 \times -3 = -12$
$-12 \div 4 = -3$
$-12 \div -3 = 4$

Do the same for these.

a $-4 \times 6 = -24$

b $3 \times -7 = -21$

c $9 \times -5 = -45$

d $-12 \times 8 = -96$

18 Copy and complete the table.

First number	36	−84	−48		72	−65		−17
Second number	−9	12		−8	−2		13	
First number ÷ second			−6	−8		5	−3	−17

19 Use the formula $m = -6n$.

a Find the value of m for these values of n.

i -1 **ii** 12 **iii** -15

iv 9 **v** -21 **vi** 14

b Some values of m are given below.
Find the value of n in the formula that would give each value of m.

i -18 **ii** -60 **iii** 72

iv 15 **v** -96 **vi** 48

Powers and roots

- Finding squares and square roots
- Cubing numbers
- Finding the cube root of a number
- Using power notation
- Using a calculator to find square roots and cube roots

Keywords

You should know

explanation 1

> Remember the correct order when you work out the value of expressions.
>
> First brackets.
> Then squares and square roots.
> Then division and multiplication.
> Finally addition and subtraction.

1 Work these out.

a 9^2

b 6^2

c 13^2

d 15^2

e $3^2 + 5^2$

f $8^2 + 7^2$

g $12^2 - 4^2$

h $4^2 + 7^2 - 3^2$

i $11^2 - 6^2 - 4^2$

j $15^2 + 5^2 - 9^2$

k 20^2

l $10^2 + 30^2$

2 Work these out.

a $\sqrt{16}$

b $\sqrt{49}$

c $\sqrt{25}$

d $\sqrt{100}$

e $\sqrt{144}$

f $\sqrt{100} + \sqrt{49}$

g $\sqrt{196} - \sqrt{64}$

h $\sqrt{81} + \sqrt{25}$

i $3^2 \times \sqrt{121}$

j $\sqrt{169} \times \sqrt{36}$

k $\sqrt{16} \times \sqrt{100}$

l $\sqrt{1600}$

3 What do you notice about the answers to question **2**, parts **k** and **l**?

4 Copy and complete these.

a $\sqrt{400} = \sqrt{(\boxed{} \times 100)} = \boxed{} \times 10 = \boxed{}$

b $\sqrt{2500} = \sqrt{(\boxed{} \times \boxed{})} = \boxed{} \times \boxed{} = \boxed{}$

c $\sqrt{6400} = \sqrt{(\boxed{} \times \boxed{})} = \boxed{} \times \boxed{} = \boxed{}$

5 Find the area of each square.

a
8 m
8 m

b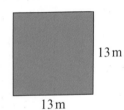
13 m
13 m

c
1.2 m
1.2 m

6 Find the length of one side of each square.

a
Area = 16 cm²

b
Area = 1 cm²

c
Area = 400 cm²

7 $2^2 = 4$. This can be written as the sum of two prime numbers: $2 + 2 = 4$.

$3^2 = 9$. This can be written as the sum of two prime numbers: $2 + 7 = 9$.

Is it possible to write every square number up to 12^2 as the sum of two prime numbers?

explanation 2

8 Here is a sequence of diagrams showing the cube numbers 1, 8, 27.

$1^3 = 1 \times 1 \times 1 = 1$ $2^3 = 2 \times 2 \times 2 = 8$ $3^3 = 3 \times 3 \times 3 = 27$

Copy and complete this table.

Number	1	2	3	4	5	6	7	8	9	10
Number cubed										

9 Work these out.

    a $3^3 + 2^3$ **b** $6^3 - 4^3$

    c $7^3 + 5^3 - 3^3$ **d** $5^3 \times 2^3$

    e half of 8^3 **f** double 10^3

    g $9^3 + 2^3$ **h** $5^3 \div 1^3$

> Remember the correct order when you work out the value of expressions.
>
> First brackets.
> Then squares, cubes, square roots and cube roots.
> Then division and multiplication.
> Finally addition and subtraction.

10 Work these out.

$$(-1)^3 = -1 \times -1 \times -1 = (-1 \times -1) \times -1 = 1 \times -1 = -1$$

    a $(-4)^3$ **b** 0.1^3 **c** $(-6)^3$ **d** 0.3^3

    e $5^3 + (-2)^3$ **f** $1^3 - 0.1^3$ **g** $(-8)^3 - (-9)^3$ **h** $0.5^3 + 0.4^3$

explanation 3

11 Work these out.

    a $\sqrt[3]{1}$ **b** $\sqrt[3]{64}$

    c $\sqrt[3]{216}$ **d** $3 \times \sqrt[3]{8}$

    e $\sqrt[3]{27} + \sqrt[3]{64}$ **f** $2 \times \sqrt[3]{512}$

    g $\sqrt[3]{1} + \sqrt[3]{343} - \sqrt[3]{125}$ **h** $\sqrt[3]{1000} \times \sqrt[3]{8}$

12 Copy and complete these.

$10 = 10^1$
$100 = 10 \times 10 = 10^2$
$1000 = \square \times \square \times \square = 10^{\square}$
$10\,000 = \square \times \square \times \square \times \square = \square^{\square}$
$100\,000 = \square \times \square \times \square \times \square \times \square = \square^{\square}$
$1\,000\,000 = \square^{\square}$

> You will find it helpful to learn these results.

    a Describe the pattern in the numbers in the left-hand column.

    b What happens to the powers of 10 as the starting numbers increase?

13 Write each expression using powers. The first one has been done for you.

   a $3 \times 3 \times 3 \times 3 = 3^4$ **b** $7 \times 7 \times 7 \times 7 \times 7$

   c $9 \times 9 \times 9 \times 9 \times 9 \times 9 \times 9 \times 9 \times 9$ **d** $13 \times 13 \times 13 \times 13$

---

explanation 4

14 Use your calculator to work these out.

   a 18^2 **b** 27^2 **c** 65^2 **d** 81^2

   e 120^2 **f** $109^2 - 96^2$ **g** $74^2 + 33^2$ **h** $55^2 - 16^2 - 39^2$

15 Use your calculator to work these out.

   a 2.5^2 **b** 5.8^2 **c** 6.1^2 **d** 8.9^2

   e 7.3^2 **f** 10.2^2 **g** 9.4^2 **h** 3.3^2

16 Use your calculator to work these out.

   a 13^3 **b** 20^3 **c** 16^3 **d** 25^3

   e 1.8^3 **f** 3.7^3 **g** 4.5^3 **h** 10.1^3

---

explanation 5

17 Copy and complete using consecutive whole numbers.

   a $\square < \sqrt{6} < \square$ **b** $\square < \sqrt{24} < \square$ **c** $\square < \sqrt{45} < \square$

   d $\square < \sqrt{88} < \square$ **e** $\square < \sqrt{152} < \square$ **f** $\square < \sqrt{200} < \square$

18 $\sqrt{8}$ lies between 2 and 3. Using only the $\boxed{x^2}$ button on your calculator it is possible to find a more accurate estimate.

Try 2.5 and continue trying other numbers to find the closest values, to 1 decimal place, to complete $\square < 8 < \square$.

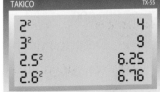

19 Use this method to find better estimates for the square roots of the numbers in question **17**.

20 Use the $\boxed{\sqrt{}}$ button on your calculator to check your answers to question **19**.

Multiples, factors and primes

- Finding lowest common multiples
- Finding highest common factors
- Finding prime factors

Keywords

You should know

explanation 1

1 a Write the first six multiples of 8.

b 112 is a multiple of 8. Write the next two multiples of 8.

2 a Write the first six multiples of 2.

b Write the first six multiples of 3.

c Which of the numbers are common multiples of 2 and 3?

d What is the lowest common multiple of 2 and 3?

3 Find the lowest common multiple of each set of numbers.

a 2, 5	**b** 4, 14	**c** 6, 9	**d** 3, 7
e 12, 15	**f** 6, 21	**g** 14, 8	**h** 9, 24
i 10, 18	**j** 3, 5, 6	**k** 4, 10, 12	**l** 5, 8, 10

4 a The lowest common multiple of two numbers is 24.
What could these numbers be?

b Find three numbers whose lowest common multiple is 36.

explanation 2

5 Write all the factors of these numbers.

a 26	**b** 32	**c** 27	**d** 40
e 48	**f** 35	**g** 56	**h** 90

6 a Is 3 a factor of these numbers?

   i 36   **ii** 56   **iii** 141   **iv** 285

   b Explain how you can tell if 3 is a factor of a large number.

7 a Is 9 a factor of these numbers?

   i 54   **ii** 72   **iii** 65   **iv** 216

   b How can you tell if 9 is a factor of a large number?

8 a Is 4 a factor of these numbers?

   i 34   **ii** 28   **iii** 132   **iv** 228

   b How can you tell if 4 is a factor of a large number?

9 a Write down all the factors of 36.

   b Write down all the factors of 64.

   c Write down the factors that are common to 36 and 64.

   d What is the highest common factor of 36 and 64?

10 Find the highest common factor of each set of numbers.

   a 16, 24   **b** 27, 63   **c** 40, 52

   d 28, 42   **e** 70, 84   **f** 72, 96

   g 93, 108   **h** 68, 96   **i** 26, 65

   j 45, 63, 72   **k** 52, 65, 91   **l** 64, 84, 104

explanation 3

11 a Write the first ten prime numbers.

   b Explain why there is only one even prime number.

12 Which of these numbers are prime?

    a 13   **b** 23   **c** 31   **d** 39

    e 53   **f** 78   **g** 87   **h** 91

    i 121   **j** 147   **k** 151   **l** 173

13 Write three 2-digit prime numbers which, when their digits are reversed, are also prime.

14 Find two prime numbers with a sum of 46 and a difference of 12.

15 Is 2011 a prime number? Use a calculator to help.

> explanation 4

16 a Copy and complete these factor trees.

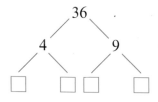
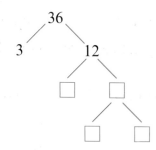

    b Write 36 as a product of its prime factors.

$$36 = \square \times \square \times \square \times \square$$
$$36 = \square \times \square$$

    c Does your answer to **b** depend on the factors you use to start the factor tree?

17 Use a factor tree to write each number as a product of its prime factors.

    a 24   **b** 45   **c** 16   **d** 60

    e 72   **f** 100·   **g** 81   **h** 48

    i 124   **j** 250   **k** 400   **l** 550

explanation 5

18 a Copy and complete these tables to find the prime factors.

i

2	84
	42
3	
	1

ii

2	180
2	
	45
•	
	1

b Use your answers to part **a** to write each number as a product of prime factors.

i $84 = \square \times \square \times \square \times \square$

   $= \square \times \square \times \square$

ii $180 = \square \times \square \times \square \times \square \times \square$

   $= \square \times \square \times \square$

19 Use the dividing method to write each of the following numbers as a product of prime factors.

a 12   **b** 36   **c** 70   **d** 81

e 120   **f** 275   **g** 105   **h** 455

20 A writing set contains one pen and one pencil.

The pens come in boxes of 10 and the pencils come in boxes of 12.

How many complete sets can be made up from these boxes?

a 1 box of pens and 1 box of pencils

b 2 boxes of pens and 3 boxes of pencils

c 3 boxes of pens and 2 boxes of pencils

Generating sequences

- Finding term-to-term rules for arithmetic sequences
- Generating a sequence from a term-to-term rule

Keywords

You should know

explanation 1

1 Each table shows patterns in a sequence.
Each term in the sequence is the number of squares in the pattern.
Copy and complete each table.

a

Pattern					
Position	1	2	3		
Term	3	5			

b

Pattern					
Position	1	2	3		
Term	1	4			

c

Pattern					
Position	1	2	3		
Term	5	8			

13

2 Copy and complete the tables to show the first five patterns in each sequence.

a

Pattern					
Position	1	2	3		
Term	3	7			

b

Pattern					
Position	1				
Term	10				

> explanation 2

3 Write the term-to-term rule for each of the sequences in questions **1** and **2**.

4 Write the term-to-term rule for each of these arithmetic sequences.

a   2   4   6   8   10

b   1   4   7   10   13

c   5   10   15   20   25

d   9   13   17   21   25

e   0.5   1   1.5   2   2.5

f   3   0   −3   −6   −9

g $\dfrac{3}{4}$ 1 $\dfrac{5}{4}$ $\dfrac{3}{2}$ $\dfrac{7}{4}$

h   4   1.5   −1   −3.5   −6

5 Write the next two terms in each of the sequences in question **4**.

6 Copy and complete the table.

	1st term	Term-to-term rule	First five terms
	0	+ 3	0, 3, 6, 9, 12
a	2	+ 5	
b	7	+ 4	
c	3	$+ \frac{1}{2}$	
d	−6	+ 4	
e	−13	+ 3	
f	8	− 5	
g	4	− 1.5	
h	1	+ 0.3	
i	1	− 0.3	
j	−0.5	+ 0.2	
k	−0.5	− 0.4	
l	$\frac{3}{4}$	$+ \frac{1}{4}$	
m	$\frac{2}{3}$	$+ \frac{1}{3}$	
n	$-\frac{2}{5}$	$+ \frac{1}{5}$	

7 a The first term of a sequence is 5. The term-to-term rule is 'add 3'.

   i What is the second term of the sequence?

   ii What is the fifth term?

  b The sixth term of a different sequence is 7. The term-to-term rule is 'subtract 2'.

   i What is the fifth term of the sequence?

   ii What is the first term?

8 Copy and complete the table.

	1st term	Term-to-term rule	2nd, 3rd, 4th and 5th terms
a	7	+5	
b		+4	9, 13, 17, 21
c			10, 16, 22, 28
d	0	−3	
e	−8		−5, −2, 1, 4
f			0.5, 1.5, 2.5, 3.5
g	1.2	−1	
h	$\dfrac{1}{2}$	$-\dfrac{1}{2}$	
i			$\dfrac{1}{5}, \dfrac{2}{5}, \dfrac{3}{5}, \dfrac{4}{5}$
j			$-\dfrac{1}{4}, -\dfrac{3}{4}, -1\dfrac{1}{4}, -1\dfrac{3}{4}$
k	0.1	+0.01	
l			1.10, 1.15, 1.20, 1.25

explanation 3

9 The first and last terms of some arithmetic sequences are given below.

   i Calculate the term-to-term rule for each sequence.

   ii Write the missing terms of each sequence.

a 3, ☐, ☐, 12

b 7, ☐, ☐, 25

c 1, ☐, ☐, ☐, 17

d 0, ☐, ☐, ☐, 20

e −3, ☐, ☐, ☐, 17

f −1, ☐, ☐, ☐, ☐, ☐, 11

g 5, ☐, ☐, ☐, −11

h 8, ☐, ☐, ☐, ☐, −12

i 2, ☐, ☐, ☐, ☐, ☐, −28

j 1, ☐, ☐, ☐, ☐, ☐, 4

k 3, ☐, ☐, ☐, ☐, 4

l −1, ☐, ☐, ☐, ☐, ☐, $\dfrac{1}{2}$

Describing sequences

- Generating a sequence from a position–to–term rule
- Writing a position–to–term rule using algebra
- Using the relationship between a term–to–term rule and a rule for the nth term

Keywords

You should know

explanation 1

1 Copy and complete the table below for each position-to-term rule.

Position	1	2	3	4	5
Term					

a Position → $+\,2$ → Term

b Position → $\times\,2$ → Term

c Position → $\times\,2$ → $+\,2$ → Term

d Position → $\times\,4$ → $-\,3$ → Term

e Position → $\times\,5$ → $+\,4$ → Term

f Position → $\times\,-2$ → $+\,1$ → Term

g Position → $\times\,-3$ → $-\,1$ → Term

h Position → $\times\,1.5$ → $-\,2$ → Term

i Position → $\times\,\frac{1}{4}$ → $+\,1$ → Term

j Position → $\div\,4$ → $+\,1$ → Term

2 What do you notice about your answers to questions **2 i** and **2 j**? Why is this?

explanation 2

3 Find the position-to-term rules for these sequences.

a

Position	1	2	3	4	5
Term	3	6	9	12	15

b

Position	1	2	3	4	5
Term	4	7	10	13	16

c

Position	1	2	3	4	5
Term	5	10	15	20	25

d

Position	1	2	3	4	5
Term	3	8	13	18	23

e

Position	1	2	3	4	5
Term	3	5	7	9	11

f

Position	1	2	3	4	5
Term	−3	−1	1	3	5

g

Position	1	2	3	4	5
Term	6	7	8	9	10

h

Position	1	2	3	4	5
Term	−4	−8	−12	−16	−20

i

Position	1	2	3	4	5
Term	−3	−7	−11	−15	−19

j

Position	1	2	3	4	5
Term	2.5	3	3.5	4	4.5

explanation 3

4 Convert these position-to-term rules into rules for the nth term.

a Position → + 3 → Term

b Position → × 4 → Term

c Position → × 2 → − 3 → Term

d Position → × 4 → − 1 → Term

e Position → × 6 → + 1 → Term

5 Convert these position-to-term rules into rules for the *n*th term.

a Position $\rightarrow$ $\boxed{\times -2}$ $\rightarrow$ $\boxed{+ 2}$ $\rightarrow$ Term

b Position $\rightarrow$ $\boxed{\times -3}$ $\rightarrow$ $\boxed{- 4}$ $\rightarrow$ Term

c Position $\rightarrow$ $\boxed{\times \frac{1}{2}}$ $\rightarrow$ $\boxed{+ 3}$ $\rightarrow$ Term

d Position $\rightarrow$ $\boxed{\div 2}$ $\rightarrow$ $\boxed{+ 3}$ $\rightarrow$ Term

e Position $\rightarrow$ $\boxed{\div 4}$ $\rightarrow$ $\boxed{- 4}$ $\rightarrow$ Term

6 These are the rules for the *n*th terms of some arithmetic sequences.
Write the first five terms of each sequence.

a $2n$ b $2n - 1$ c $3n + 4$ d $5n - 1$

e $3n - 8$ f $4n - 4$ g $\frac{1}{2} n$ h $\frac{1}{2} n + 1$

i $-2n$ j $-3n + 6$ k $-n + 1$ l $-\frac{1}{4} n + 2$

7 Each table shows an arithmetic sequence.

  i Write the term-to-term rule for each sequence.

  ii Write the rule for the *n*th term of each sequence.

a

Position	1	2	3	4	5
Term	4	8	12	16	20

b

Position	1	2	3	4	5
Term	5	9	13	17	21

c

Position	1	2	3	4	5
Term	3	6	9	12	15

d

Position	1	2	3	4	5
Term	1	4	7	10	13

e

Position	1	2	3	4	5
Term	7	9	11	13	15

f

Position	1	2	3	4	5
Term	-3	-1	1	3	5

8 Each table shows an arithmetic sequence.

Write the term-to-term rule and the nth term of each sequence.

a

Position	1	2	3	4	5
Term	−2	−4	−6	−8	−10

b

Position	1	2	3	4	5
Term	−4	−6	−8	−10	−12

c

Position	1	2	3	4	5
Term	$-\frac{1}{2}$	0	$\frac{1}{2}$	1	$1\frac{1}{2}$

9 What do you notice about the term-to-term rules and the rules for the nth terms for the arithmetic sequences in questions **7** and **8**?

10 Copy and complete these sentences.

a   The rule for the nth term is $3n + 1$. The term-to-term rule is ...

b   The rule for the nth term is $4n + 6$. The term-to-term rule is ...

c   The rule for the nth term is $2n - 8$. The term-to-term rule is ...

d   The rule for the nth term is $-3n + 1$. The term-to-term rule is ...

e   The rule for the nth term is $-5n - 2$. The term-to-term rule is ...

f   The term-to-term rule is $+ 2$. A possible rule for the nth term is ...

g   The term-to-term rule is $+ 8$. A possible rule for the nth term is ...

h   The term-to-term rule is $- 7$. A possible rule for the nth term is ...

i   The term-to-term rule is $+ \frac{1}{2}$. A possible rule for the nth term is ...

j   The term-to-term rule is $- \frac{1}{4}$. A possible rule for the nth term is ...

11 Write the rule for the nth term of these arithmetic sequences.

a   4, 5, 6, 7, 8   b   10, 15, 20, 25, 30   c   −2, 1, 4, 7, 10

d   12, 22, 32, 42, 52   e   7, 13, 19, 25, 31   f   −3, 2, 7, 12, 17

g   0, −1, −2, −3, −4   h   6, 4, 2, 0, −2   i   −5.5, −5, −4.5, −4, −3.5

Angles

- Identifying alternate and corresponding angles
- Proving that the angles of a triangle add up to 180° and that the angles of any quadrilateral add up to 360°
- Knowing that the exterior angle of a triangle is equal to the sum of the two interior opposite angles

Keywords

You should know

explanation 1a   explanation 1b   explanation 1c

1 a Look at this diagram.

Give a reason why each of these statements is true.

i   angle p = angle r

ii angle p = angle t

iii angle r = angle t

iv angle q = angle s

v   angle q = angle u

vi angle s = angle u

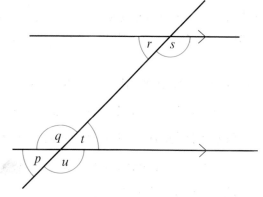

b Look at this diagram.

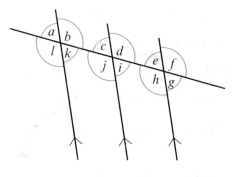

List all the pairs of

i   alternate angles

ii vertically opposite angles

iii corresponding angles

2 Calculate the size of each angle marked by a letter.
Give reasons for your answers.

a

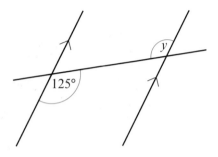

b

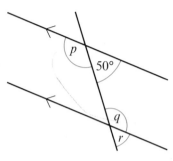

c

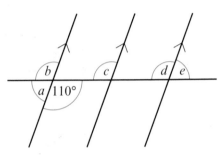

d

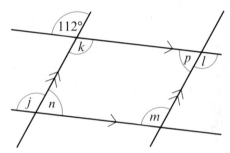

(explanation 2a) (explanation 2b)

3 Calculate the size of each angle marked by a letter. Give reasons for your answers.

a

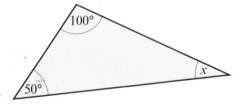

b

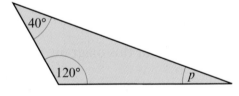

c

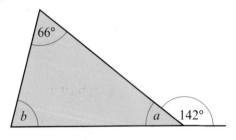

d

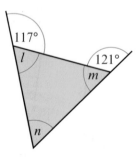

4 Calculate the size of each angle marked by a letter.
Give reasons for your answers.

a

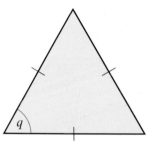

b

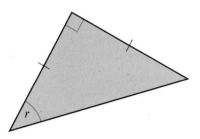

explanation 3a   explanation 3b

5 Calculate the size of each angle marked by a letter.
Give reasons for your answers.

a

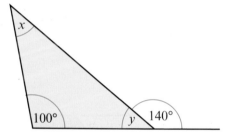

b

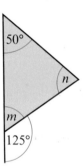

c

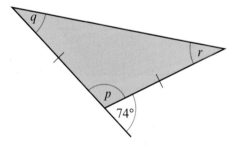

d

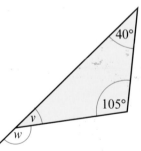

e

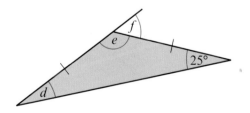

f

explanation 4

6 Calculate the size of each angle marked by a letter.
Give reasons for your answers.

a

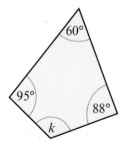

b

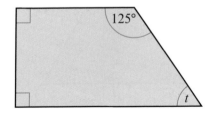

c

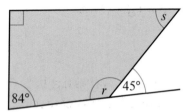

d

e

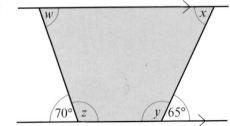

f

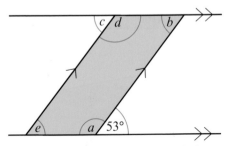

7 Calculate the size of each angle marked by a letter.
Give reasons for your answers.

a

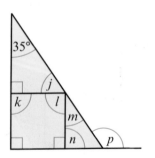

b

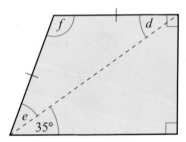

Lines, shapes and coordinates

- Classifying quadrilaterals by their geometric properties
- Calculating the midpoint of a line segment

Keywords

You should know

explanation 1

1 Look at this flow chart. It shows a possible way to classify quadrilaterals.

  a The boxes labelled **A** shold both contain the same question.
  What question should they contain?

  b What is the name of quadrilateral **B**?

  c One of the categories in this classification is 'Other quadrilaterals'.
  Name three types of quadrilaterals that are included in this category.

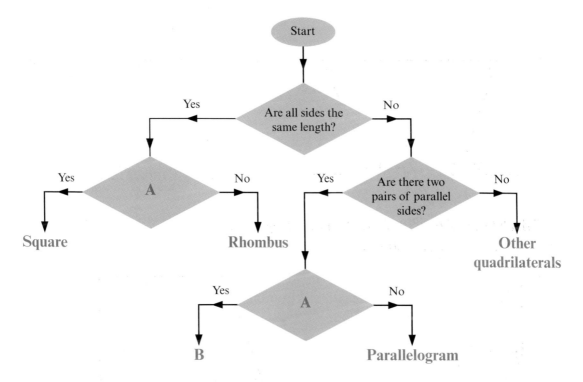

2 a For each property below, name all of the types of quadrilateral shown that *always* have that property.

   i All sides are the same length.

   ii All angles are the same size.

  iii Opposite sides are equal.

  iv Opposite angles are equal.

   v There are two pairs of parallel sides.

  vi There is only one pair of parallel sides.

 vii Diagonals are of the same length.

viii The diagonals intersect at right angles.

  ix There is only one line of reflection symmetry.

   x It has rotational symmetry of order 2.

  xi There are at least two lines of reflection symmetry.

 xii There are four lines of reflection symmetry.

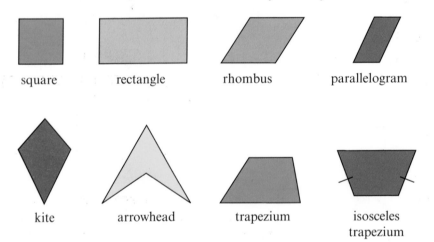

square   rectangle   rhombus   parallelogram

kite   arrowhead   trapezium   isosceles trapezium

b **i** Which property from part **a** do all trapeziums have?

   ii Which of the properties do all rhombuses have, but squares never have?

3 In each grid, three vertices of a quadrilateral are plotted.
What are the coordinates of the fourth vertex?

a A square

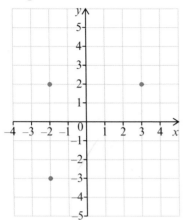

b A rhombus

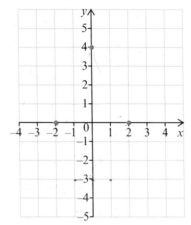

c A rectangle

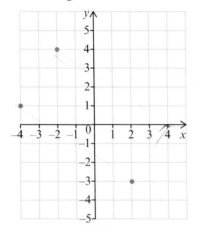

d A kite

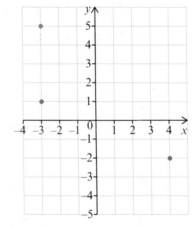

e A rhombus

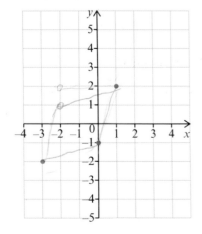

f An arrowhead

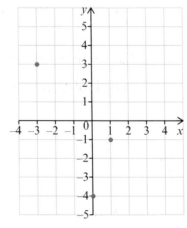

27

explanation 2a   explanation 2b   explanation 2c

4 Write the coordinates of the midpoint of each line segment.

a
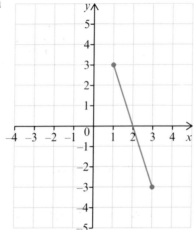

b
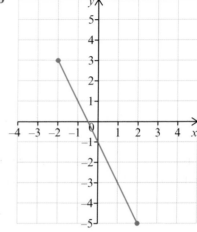

c
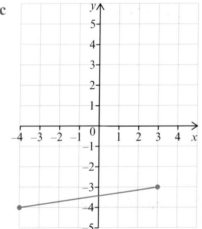

d
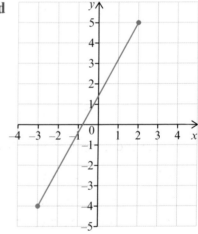

5 These are the coordinates of the end points of line segments.
Calculate the coordinates of the midpoint of each line segment.

a   (2, 4) and (4, 8)   b   (0, 2) and (6, 2)   c   (−6, 1) and (2, 0)

d   (−4, 2) and (0, −4)   e   (1, −3) and (0, 0)   f   (2, −3) and (−1, 6)

6 Point M is the midpoint of line segment AB. The coordinates of points A and
M are given. In each case, calculate the coordinates of point B.

a   A(1, 2), M(5, 3)   b   A(−2, 1), M(4, −1)   c   A(3, −8), M(1, −4)

Constructions (1)

- Constructing a perpendicular bisector
- Bisecting an angle
- Constructing a perpendicular from a point to a line
- Constructing a perpendicular from a point on a line

Keywords

You should know

explanation 1a explanation 1b explanation 1c explanation 1d

1 Practise using a pair of compasses to construct perpendicular bisectors of lines that are not horizontal or vertical.

Make sure you are confident that you can do this type of construction well.

2 Using a ruler and pencil, draw triangle ABC on squared paper.

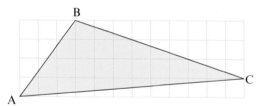

a Construct the perpendicular bisector of side AB.

b Construct the perpendicular bisector of side BC.

c What do you notice about the distance of the point of intersection of the two perpendicular bisectors from A, B and C?

3 The map shows a shoreline.

Three people stand at A, B and C. They each see a boat out at sea. The boat is equidistant from each of the three people.
Copy the diagram. By construction, locate the position of the boat.

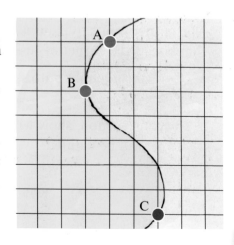

Use what you found out in question **2c** to help you.

explanation 2a   explanation 2b   explanation 2c   explanation 2d

4 Practise using a pair of compasses to construct angle bisectors.

Bisect angles of different sizes, for example some acute and some obtuse.

Make sure you are confident that you can do this type of construction well.

5 This question is about bisecting angles.

   a Using a protractor, draw an angle of 70°.

   b By construction, bisect the angle.

   c Using a protractor, check that the angle has been bisected.

6 Draw triangle XYZ on squared paper.

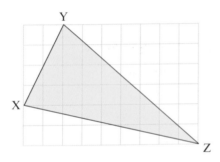

   a By construction, bisect angle X.

   b By construction, bisect angles Y and Z.

   c What do you notice about the three angle bisectors?

7 The diagram shows a field PQRS.

The farmer wants to plant a hedge that bisects the corner of his field at P.

   a Copy the diagram onto squared paper.

   b By construction, show where the hedge will be planted.

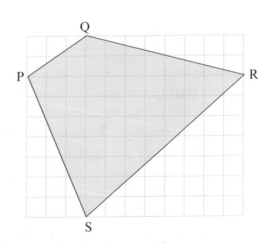

explanation 3a   explanation 3b   explanation 3c   explanation 3d

8 Practise using a pair of compasses to construct the perpendicular from a point to a line that is not horizontal or vertical.
Make sure you are confident that you can do this type of construction well.

9 Copy this diagram onto squared paper.

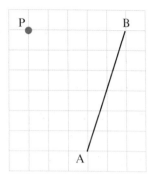

  a Construct the shortest line segment from P to the line AB.

  Label the point where the two lines meet Q.

  b You can construct an angle of 45° by bisecting a right angle.

  Without using a protractor, mark and label a point R so that angle PQR = 45° and PQ = QR.

10 Copy triangle ABC onto centimetre squared paper.

Check that the length of side BC is 5 cm.

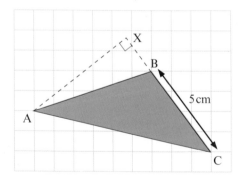

  a Line segment AX is perpendicular to side BC.

  Construct the line segment AX and measure its length.

  b The area of the triangle is given by

  $\frac{1}{2} \times$ length BC $\times$ length AX

  Use your answer to part **a** to calculate the area of the triangle.

11 Using a ruler and protractor, copy the parallelogram WXYZ below.

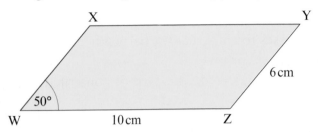

a By construction, bisect angle WZY.

b Mark a point, P, 4 cm from Z on the line constructed in part **a**.

c Construct the shortest line from P to the line WZ. Measure its length.

d Construct the shortest line from P to YZ. Measure its length.

explanation 4a   explanation 4b   explanation 4c

12 Practise using a pair of compasses to construct a perpendicular from a point on a line that is not horizontal or vertical.

Make sure you are confident that you can do this type of construction well.

13 Follow the instructions to draw a diagram. Make a sketch first.

a Draw a line AB 7 cm long. Mark a point X on it so that AX = 5 cm.

b Construct a perpendicular to the line AB, passing through X. Label the line XY.

c Mark a point C on XY so that XC = 8 cm.

d Draw the triangle ABC. Measure the lengths AC and BC.

14 Follow the instructions to draw a diagram. Make a sketch first.

a Draw a line PQ 8 cm long. Mark two points X and Y on it so that PX = 3 cm and PY = 5 cm.

b Construct perpendiculars to the line PQ, passing through X and Y. Label the lines WX and YZ.

c Mark a point S on WX so that XS = 4 cm.

d Mark a point R on YZ so that YR = 4 cm.

e Draw the quadrilateral PQRS. What type of quadrilateral is PQRS?

f Measure the lengths PS and QR.

Chance and probability

- Recognising certain and impossible outcomes and stating their probabilities
- Calculating the probability of an event for equally likely outcomes
- Understanding that random processes are unpredictable

Keywords

You should know

explanation 1a   explanation 1b

1 Write down the probability of each event.

 a The sun will set tomorrow.

 b You will have only one birthday next year.

 c Tomorrow will be Sunday.

2 Describe an event with each probability.

 a The event is impossible.

 b The event has an even chance of happening.

 c The event is certain to happen.

3 a List all the outcomes when rolling a fair six-sided dice.

 b Are these outcomes equally likely?

 c Explain your answer to part **b**.

4 a What is probability of rolling a six with the dice in question **3**?

 b If you rolled the dice six times, how many sixes would you expect?

 c If you rolled the dice sixty times, how many sixes would you expect?

 d Are you guaranteed to get exactly the number of sixes you expected?

 e Give a reason for your answer to part **d**.

5 A card game uses a set of ten different digit cards.

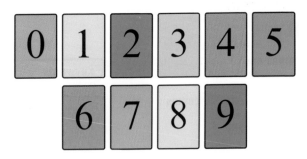

    a A card is chosen at random. How many possible outcomes are there?

    b What is the probability that the card chosen shows an odd number?

    c What is the probability that the card chosen shows a prime number?

    d What is the probability of choosing a card that shows a multiple of 8?

    e What is the probability of choosing a card that shows a factor of 36?

6 A class chooses their school council rep by writing the name of every member of the class on a piece of paper, putting the pieces of paper into a box and then drawing out one name. There are 14 girls and 15 boys in the class.

    a How many possible outcomes are there?

    b What is the probability that a boy will be chosen as the rep?

    c Anna was the rep last term. What is the probability she will be chosen again?

    d Do you think this is a good way to choose a rep from the class?

7 Three different scratch cards, A, B and C, all have some shaded squares as shown below. All 12 squares on each card are hidden, and you may reveal just one square on each card.

    a On which card are you most likely to reveal a hidden shaded square?

    b Explain your answer to part **a**.

    A   B   C

8 Design your own set of three scratch cards and state which one you should choose to increase your chance of success.

9 Sarah has thrown a head eight times in a row with her 10p coin and predicts that she will throw a head again next time.

   a Do you think she is right?

   b Is there enough evidence to say that the coin is biased?

10 Work with a partner.

Take a set of ten different digit cards, shuffle them and lay them face down in a line.

The first player turns over the first card.

Before the second player turns over the second card both write down whether you think this card will be higher or lower than the first card, giving a reason for your answer. You get a point for a correct prediction.

Taking turns, continue in the same way with the rest of the cards.

A rich Frenchman, the Chevalier de Mere, played a gambling game in which he bet that he could throw a six in four throws of a dice. He also bet that with two dice he could throw a double six in 24 throws.

He invited the philosopher and mathematician Blaise Pascal to work out the true probabilities of these outcomes.

Try to find out more about Pascal's work.

Probability

- Finding the probability of an event not occurring
- Using diagrams to record all possible outcomes for a single event
- Using diagrams to record all possible outcomes for two successive events

Keywords

You should know

explanation 1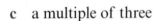

1 A bag contains two red counters, three blue counters and three green counters. A counter is taken out of the bag at random.

a Find, as a fraction, the probability of these outcomes.

i a red counter

ii a blue counter

iii a green counter

iv either a red or a blue counter

b Add together your answers for i, ii and iii. Explain your result.

2 A game uses a ten-sided dice, numbered from 1 to 10. Give, as decimals, the probabilities for these events when the dice is rolled.

a a seven

b an even number

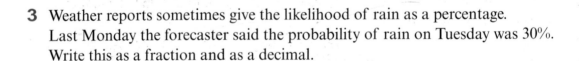

c a multiple of three

d a factor of twelve

e a prime number

3 Weather reports sometimes give the likelihood of rain as a percentage. Last Monday the forecaster said the probability of rain on Tuesday was 30%. Write this as a fraction and as a decimal.

4 There are ten counters in a bag. Five are blue, three are red and two are yellow. One counter is taken from the bag at random. Find the probability of selecting each colour. Write the probability as a fraction, a decimal and a percentage.

a red

b yellow

c blue

explanation 2a   explanation 2b

5 a What is the probability of throwing a 6 with a fair six-sided dice?

b What is the probability of throwing a number less than 6?

c Describe two ways in which you could work out the answer to part **b**.

6 A set of snooker balls consists of 15 red balls and one each of yellow, green, brown, blue, pink, black and white.

One ball is chosen at random. Find the probability of these outcomes.

a red

b not red

c green

d not green

e either blue or pink

7 Work out the probability that this spinner will land on these colours.

a yellow

b blue

c green

d either blue or green

e not blue

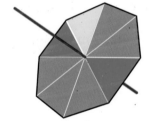

8 There are 45 cars in the school car park. 15 are silver, 9 are red, 6 are blue, 5 are white and the rest are black. Calculate the probability that the first car to leave will be this colour.

a silver

b white

c neither silver nor white

d black or blue

9 You have a pack of 52 playing cards and deal one card from the pack.

Work out the probability of dealing these cards.

a a red card	There are four suits in a pack of cards: hearts and diamonds which are red; clubs and spades which are black.
b a heart	
c not a heart	Each suit contains an Ace, 2, 3, 4, 5, 6, 7, 8, 9, 10, jack, queen and king.
d either a spade or a diamond	
e not a queen	The picture cards are jack, queen and king.
f not a picture card	

10 Mike travels to school by bus. The probability that the bus is on time is 0.82.

   a   What is the probability that the bus is not on time?

   b   Will the probability that the bus is late be the same as your answer to part **a**? Explain.

11 The probability that Lucy hands her homework in on time is 0.75. The probability that she hands it in early is 0.1. What is the probability that she hands her homework in late?

12 A letter is chosen at random from the word MATHEMATICS.

   a   How many possible outcomes are there?

   b   What is the probability that the letter is M?

   c   What is the probability that the letter is either A, E or I?

   d   What is the probability that the letter is not T?

(explanation 3)

13 Draw a table to show all the possible outcomes when two coins are spun. Use your table to find the probabilities of these events.

   a   Two tails are thrown.

   b   Both coins land the same way up.

14 On Monday the canteen offered pasta bake, chicken korma or veggie burgers. For pudding the choice was fruit salad or sponge pudding. Ian has one main course and one pudding. Draw a table to show all the possible meals he could choose.

Main course	Pudding

15 A cooked breakfast is available each morning. Pupils can choose any two of these items: sausage, bacon, scrambled eggs and beans. Write all the different breakfasts you could choose.

16 A glazier can put red, green or blue glass in each of two windows. List all the possible ways he can glaze the two windows.

17 Amy spins a coin and rolls a dice. Some of the possible outcomes are shown on this sample space diagram.

		Dice					
		1	2	3	4	5	6
Coin	H	H, 1	H, 2				
	T				T, 4		T, 6

  a Copy and complete the diagram.

  b What is the total number of outcomes?

  c What is the probability of getting a head and a 5?

  d What is the probability of getting a tail and a number less than 4?

  e What is the probability of getting a 2?

18 A red and a blue dice, each numbered from 1 to 6, are rolled and the scores are added together.

	•	••	•••	••••	•••••	••••••
•	2					
••				7		
•••			6			
••••					10	
•••••				9		
••••••	8					

a Copy and complete the sample space diagram to show all the possible outcomes.

b Which outcome is most likely?

c Use the diagram to find the probability of these events.

   i The same number on both dice.

   ii The sum of the numbers is less than 10.

   iii The score on the red dice is exactly double the score on the blue dice.

19 Neera has a 2p coin, a 10p coin and a 20p coin. She spins each of them and records whether they land head up or tail up.

a List all the possible outcomes.

b Use your list to find the probability of these events.

   i All three coins land head up.

   ii No coins land head up.

   iii At least one coin lands head up.

20 Two four-sided dice, each numbered 1, 2, 3 and 4, are rolled, and the numbers scored are multiplied together.

a Draw a sample space diagram to show all the possible outcomes.

b Use your diagram to find the probability of these events.

   i an even number

   ii an odd number

   iii a multiple of 3

   iv a factor of 24

Experimental probability

- Using experimental data to estimate probabilities
- Understanding the effect of repeating an experiment many times
- Comparing theoretical and experimental probabilities

Keywords

You should know

explanation 1

1 Work with a partner.

You need a bag containing a small selection of different coloured counters or cubes. Take one counter/cube from the bag and note its colour before replacing it. Do this 10 times. Now estimate the probability of each colour in the bag. Check by emptying the bag and counting the number of counters/cubes of each colour.

2 If, in question **1**, you selected a counter/cube from the bag 50 times would you be able to make a more reliable prediction?

3 The lifetimes of 500 light bulbs are given in the table.

Lifetime	Frequency
0−99 hours	150
100−199 hours	300
200−299 hours	50

If I buy a similar bulb, what is the probability that it will last at least 200 hours?

4 Avnee has cards numbered 1, 2, 3, 4 or 5. She puts several cards in a bag. She takes out a random card, records the number on the card and then replaces it in the bag. The table shows her results.

Number on Card	1	2	3	4	5
Tally	ꖌꖌꖌꖌꖌ l	lll	ll	ꖌꖌꖌꖌꖌ lll	ꖌꖌꖌꖌꖌ
Frequency					

a Copy the table and complete the last row.

b How many times did Avnee take a card out of the bag?

c Which number did she take out most often?

d Estimate the probability that the next card Avnee picks has the number 2 on it.

5 You need a four-sided dice numbered from 1 to 4. If you do not have one, you can make one using a net like the one shown.

a What is the probability of rolling a 4 with your four-sided dice?

b Roll your dice 20 times and record the result each time. Comment on your results.

c Now roll the dice another 20 times and combine both sets of results. How have the results changed?

6 a Roll two four-sided dice and add together the scores. Do this 30 times and record the results in a frequency diagram.

b Work out the relative frequency of each outcome. Compare your results with those of someone else in your class. Are the results different? Why do you think this happens?

c What do you think might happen to the results if you repeat the experiment?

Carry out the experiment another 20 times and record these scores on your diagram.

What effect do the extra throws have on the results? Is this what you expected?

explanation 2

7 The table shows the results in the Premiership at one stage in the football season.

Home wins	24
Away wins	9
Draws	4

a Use the data in the table to estimate the probability of getting the following results in a randomly selected match taking place the next week. Give each answer as a decimal rounded to 2 decimal places.

    i a home win

    ii an away win

    iii a draw

These were the results much later in the season.

Home wins	145
Away wins	79
Draws	76

b Calculate the probability of each outcome, as a decimal rounded to 2 decimal places, based on the final table.

c Will your answers to part **a** or part **b** be more reliable? Why?

43

explanation 3 ───

8 a Roll two dice 40 times. Record the total score and represent the different outcomes on a frequency diagram. Calculate the experimental probability of each score.

   b Draw a sample space diagram showing all the possible scores. Calculate the theoretical probability of each score.

   Comment on the differences or similarities between the theoretical and the experimental probabilities.

   c Describe how the experimental results would change if you increase the number of trials.

9 Ravi bought a combination padlock for his sports locker. He knows the last three digits of the code are 850, but he cannot remember the first digit, which is a number from 0 to 9.

   a What is the probability that he will choose the correct number on his first attempt?

   b Design and carry out an experiment to calculate an experimental probability for Ravi's problem.

   c Compare your answer with the theoretical probability.

10 In the National Lottery there are 49 balls numbered from 1 to 49.

   a What is the probability of these events for the first ball picked?

   i an even number

   ii a prime number

   iii a multiple of 6

   iv a number greater than 35

   b Design and carry out an experiment to test the theoretical probabilities.

11 Drop 5 multilink cubes onto your desk and record, in a table, whether each lands bump up, bump to the side, or tilted with bump down. Repeat this 10 times so that you have 50 results. Collate the results from everyone in your class. Compare your results with the total class results.

Fractions and decimals

- Using division to convert fractions to decimals
- Understanding that a recurring decimal is a fraction
- Ordering fractions

Keywords

You should know

explanation 1

1 Write each decimal as a fraction in its lowest terms.

    a 0.8   **b** 0.45   **c** 0.72   **d** 0.98

    e 0.125   **f** 0.255   **g** 0.312   **h** 0.782

2 Change these decimals to mixed numbers and simplify as far as possible.

    a 2.75   **b** 14.35   **c** 55.55   **d** 36.625

    e 79.235   **f** 124.452   **g** 163.128   **h** 201.402

explanation 2a   explanation 2b

3 Use division to change these fractions to decimals.

    a $\dfrac{1}{5}$ **b** $\dfrac{1}{10}$ **c** $\dfrac{3}{8}$

    d $\dfrac{2}{5}$ **e** $\dfrac{7}{8}$ **f** $\dfrac{9}{5}$

    g $\dfrac{23}{4}$ **h** $\dfrac{37}{8}$ **i** $\dfrac{31}{4}$

4 Use a calculator to write each fraction as a decimal.

    a $\dfrac{1}{40}$ **b** $\dfrac{1}{16}$ **c** $\dfrac{3}{80}$

    d $\dfrac{3}{32}$ **e** $\dfrac{5}{16}$ **f** $\dfrac{36}{32}$

    g $\dfrac{66}{40}$ **h** $\dfrac{99}{45}$ **i** $\dfrac{142}{64}$

5 This table shows the time Amy spent on homework last week.

Subject	Maths	English	Science	History	Geography	RS	French	Art	Music
Minutes	50	45	55	30	30	15	35	20	20

    a What was the total time Amy spent on homework last week?

    b What fraction of that time did she spend on each subject?

    c Use a calculator to change each fraction in part **b** into a decimal.

6 a Write $\frac{1}{3}$ as a decimal using a calculator.

    b What do you notice about the answer on the calculator display?

    c Write down what you think $\frac{2}{3}$ will be as a decimal.

    d Check your answer using a calculator.

    e Predict the decimal forms of $\frac{3}{3}, \frac{4}{3}, \frac{5}{3}, \frac{6}{3}$ and $\frac{7}{3}$.

    f Check your answers using a calculator.

7 Use a calculator to find the decimal equivalents of $\frac{1}{6}, \frac{1}{9}, \frac{1}{11}$ and $\frac{1}{12}$.

8 a Convert each fraction to a decimal.

    i $\frac{1}{2}$ **ii** $\frac{2}{3}$ **iii** $\frac{3}{7}$

    iv $\frac{7}{9}$ **v** $\frac{5}{11}$ **vi** $\frac{6}{15}$

    vii $\frac{7}{16}$ **viii** $\frac{11}{12}$ **ix** $\frac{14}{24}$

    b **i** Which fractions in part **a** give terminating decimals?

        ii Which fractions in part **a** give recurring decimals?

9 Write three recurring decimals and their equivalent fractions.

explanation 3

10 i Write both fractions in each pair with a common denominator.

    ii Which of the original fractions is bigger?

    a $\dfrac{6}{10}, \dfrac{2}{5}$ **b** $\dfrac{3}{7}, \dfrac{4}{6}$ **c** $\dfrac{7}{8}, \dfrac{4}{5}$ **d** $\dfrac{14}{12}, \dfrac{6}{5}$

11 i Write the fractions in each group with a common denominator.

    ii Write the original fractions in order of size, smallest first.

    a $\dfrac{1}{4}, \dfrac{1}{5}, \dfrac{1}{6}$ **b** $\dfrac{3}{5}, \dfrac{2}{3}, \dfrac{1}{2}$ **c** $\dfrac{5}{8}, \dfrac{4}{7}, \dfrac{2}{3}$ **d** $\dfrac{7}{12}, \dfrac{9}{16}, \dfrac{13}{20}$

12 Convert the fractions in each group in question **11** to decimals. Use these to check the orders in part **ii**.

13 Copy this number line.

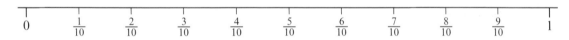

    Mark these fractions on the number line.

    a $\dfrac{2}{5}$ **b** $\dfrac{1}{3}$ **c** $\dfrac{4}{7}$ **d** $\dfrac{6}{20}$ **e** $\dfrac{7}{12}$

14 Which number in each pair is greater?

    a 0.21 or $\dfrac{3}{16}$ **b** 0.25 or $\dfrac{4}{15}$ **c** 0.36 or $\dfrac{8}{23}$ **d** 0.78 or $\dfrac{27}{34}$

15 i Write each pair of fractions with a common denominator.

    ii Work out the fraction that is exactly halfway between the pair.

    a $\dfrac{2}{5}$ and $\dfrac{4}{9}$ **b** $\dfrac{3}{5}$ and $\dfrac{5}{7}$ **c** $\dfrac{1}{2}$ and $\dfrac{3}{5}$ **d** $\dfrac{2}{3}$ and $\dfrac{7}{8}$

Calculations with fractions

- Adding and subtracting fractions with different denominators
- Multiplying and dividing whole numbers by fractions

Keywords

You should know

explanation 1

1 Work these out, giving each answer in its lowest terms.

a $\dfrac{4}{7} + \dfrac{2}{7}$
b $\dfrac{3}{5} - \dfrac{1}{5}$
c $\dfrac{2}{13} + \dfrac{5}{13}$
d $\dfrac{3}{16} + \dfrac{5}{16}$

e $\dfrac{7}{18} - \dfrac{1}{18}$
f $\dfrac{8}{21} - \dfrac{5}{21}$
g $\dfrac{7}{25} + \dfrac{14}{25}$
h $\dfrac{19}{30} - \dfrac{11}{30}$

i $\dfrac{13}{15} - \dfrac{4}{15}$
j $\dfrac{5}{18} + \dfrac{7}{18}$
k $\dfrac{7}{20} + \dfrac{9}{20}$
l $\dfrac{13}{24} - \dfrac{7}{24}$

2 Copy and complete.

 + 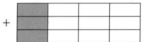 =

$\dfrac{2}{3} + \dfrac{1}{4} = \dfrac{\square}{12} + \dfrac{\square}{12} = \dfrac{\square + \square}{12} = \dfrac{\square}{12}$

3 Work these out.

a $\dfrac{1}{5} + \dfrac{7}{10}$
b $\dfrac{3}{8} + \dfrac{1}{4}$
c $\dfrac{5}{12} + \dfrac{1}{6}$
d $\dfrac{2}{7} + \dfrac{3}{14}$

e $\dfrac{3}{8} + \dfrac{9}{16}$
f $\dfrac{5}{6} + \dfrac{1}{12}$
g $\dfrac{3}{10} + \dfrac{12}{20}$
h $\dfrac{7}{16} + \dfrac{3}{8}$

4 Work these out.

a $\dfrac{1}{4} + \dfrac{2}{3}$
b $\dfrac{1}{6} + \dfrac{5}{9}$
c $\dfrac{1}{3} + \dfrac{3}{5}$
d $\dfrac{2}{7} + \dfrac{1}{4}$

e $\dfrac{2}{5} + \dfrac{1}{3}$
f $\dfrac{3}{7} + \dfrac{2}{5}$
g $\dfrac{7}{12} + \dfrac{5}{18}$
h $\dfrac{11}{15} + \dfrac{4}{25}$

5 Copy and complete.

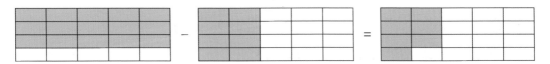

$$\frac{3}{4} - \frac{2}{5} = \frac{\square}{20} - \frac{\square}{20} = \frac{\square - \square}{20} = \frac{\square}{20}$$

6 Work these out.

a $\dfrac{7}{12} - \dfrac{1}{6}$ b $\dfrac{3}{4} - \dfrac{5}{8}$ c $\dfrac{13}{16} - \dfrac{5}{8}$ d $\dfrac{4}{5} - \dfrac{7}{10}$

e $\dfrac{13}{18} - \dfrac{4}{9}$ f $\dfrac{4}{5} - \dfrac{7}{20}$ g $\dfrac{2}{3} - \dfrac{11}{18}$ h $\dfrac{23}{24} - \dfrac{5}{6}$

7 Work these out. Give your answers in their lowest terms.

a $\dfrac{8}{9} - \dfrac{1}{2}$ b $\dfrac{3}{5} - \dfrac{1}{4}$ c $\dfrac{2}{3} - \dfrac{2}{7}$ d $\dfrac{5}{8} - \dfrac{1}{3}$

e $\dfrac{5}{6} - \dfrac{7}{10}$ f $\dfrac{7}{8} - \dfrac{2}{3}$ g $\dfrac{4}{5} - \dfrac{3}{8}$ h $\dfrac{5}{6} - \dfrac{3}{4}$

explanation 2

8 Work these out and simplify your answers.

a $\dfrac{1}{3} + \dfrac{4}{5}$ b $\dfrac{6}{7} + \dfrac{1}{4}$ c $\dfrac{5}{12} + \dfrac{5}{8}$ d $\dfrac{4}{5} + \dfrac{3}{7}$

e $\dfrac{5}{6} + \dfrac{3}{7}$ f $1\dfrac{2}{5} + \dfrac{7}{9}$ g $\dfrac{5}{7} + 1\dfrac{1}{3}$ h $2\dfrac{1}{2} + \dfrac{4}{5}$

9 Work these out and simplify your answers.

a $1 - \dfrac{4}{15}$ b $1\dfrac{3}{8} - \dfrac{3}{4}$ c $1\dfrac{1}{5} - \dfrac{7}{10}$ d $1\dfrac{7}{12} - \dfrac{2}{3}$

e $1\dfrac{1}{3} - \dfrac{1}{2}$ f $1\dfrac{1}{4} - \dfrac{2}{3}$ g $1\dfrac{2}{5} - \dfrac{1}{2}$ h $1\dfrac{3}{4} - \dfrac{5}{6}$

10 Although early Egyptians used fractions like $\frac{1}{2}, \frac{1}{3}, \frac{1}{4}$ and so on, they did not

have notation to write fractions such as $\frac{2}{3}, \frac{4}{5}$ or $\frac{2}{11}$.

The fractions they used all have a numerator of one and are called unit fractions. The Egyptians were able to write any fraction as a sum of unit fractions. For example,

$$\frac{3}{8} = \frac{2}{8} + \frac{1}{8} = \frac{1}{4} + \frac{1}{8} \qquad \frac{5}{12} = \frac{1}{4} + \frac{1}{6} \qquad \frac{7}{9} = \frac{1}{2} + \frac{1}{4} + \frac{1}{36}$$

Write these fractions as Egyptian fractions.

a $\frac{5}{8}$ b $\frac{7}{12}$ c $\frac{13}{15}$ d $\frac{9}{20}$ e $\frac{17}{30}$

---

explanation 3

11 Work these out.

a $\frac{2}{3}$ of 18   b $\frac{2}{5}$ of £240   c $\frac{3}{8}$ of 160 g   d $\frac{4}{7}$ of 50 kg

e three quarters of 75   f five ninths of 30

g $\frac{5}{12}$ of 100 cm   h $\frac{5}{6}$ of 84p

12 This pie chart shows the colours of 80 cars in a car park.

a $\frac{1}{4}$ of the cars are silver.
How many silver cars are there?

b $\frac{3}{8}$ of the cars are red.
How many red cars are there?

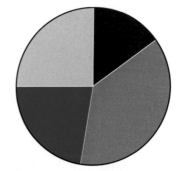

c There are 12 black cars.
What fraction of the total
number of cars is this?

d How many blue cars are there?

e What fraction of the cars are blue?

f The sum of the angles at the centre of the pie chart is 360°.
Find the angle for each sector.

explanation 4a explanation 4b

13 Work these out.

a $\dfrac{2}{7} \times 14$ b $\dfrac{4}{6} \times 24$ c $\dfrac{7}{12} \times 84$ d $\dfrac{7}{8} \times 16$

e $\dfrac{2}{3} \times 16$ f $\dfrac{5}{7} \times 30$ g $1\dfrac{3}{5} \times 6$ h $1\dfrac{2}{9} \times 7$

14 Find these amounts.

a $\dfrac{5}{6} \times 36\,\text{kg}$ b $1\dfrac{1}{9} \times 18\,\text{m}$ c $\dfrac{7}{12} \times 36\,\text{kg}$

d $1\dfrac{2}{3} \times 33\,\text{cm}$ e $2\dfrac{1}{2} \times 50\,\text{mm}$ f $1\dfrac{4}{5} \times 120\,\text{g}$

15 Copy and complete.

$3 \times 4 = \square$

$2 \times 4 = \square$

$1 \times 4 = \square$

$\dfrac{1}{2} \times 4 = \square$

$\dfrac{1}{3} \times 4 = \square$

explanation 5

16 a How many sevenths are there in this rectangle?

b How many thirds are there in this circle?

51

17 a How many thirds
are there in these
four circles?

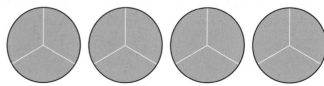

   b How many sixths are there
in these three prisms?

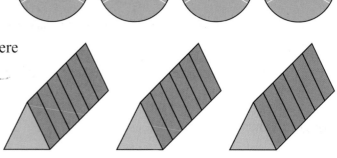

18 a How many quarters are there in 20?

   b Copy and complete this number sentence. $20 = \square \times \frac{1}{4}$

19 Copy and complete this sentence.

Dividing by $\frac{1}{5}$ is the same as multiplying by $\square$.

20 Work these out.

   a $10 \div \frac{1}{2}$ **b** $9 \div \frac{1}{3}$ **c** $12 \div \frac{1}{5}$ **d** $20 \div \frac{1}{7}$

   e $8 \div \frac{1}{4}$ **f** $15 \div \frac{1}{6}$ **g** $3 \div \frac{1}{10}$ **h** $1 \div \frac{1}{12}$

21 Copy and complete these sentences.

   a $30 \times \frac{1}{5} = \square$ therefore $\square \div \frac{1}{5} = 30$

   b $15 \times \frac{2}{5} = \square$ therefore $\square \div \frac{2}{5} = 15$

   c $\square \times \frac{3}{5} = 6$ therefore $6 \div \frac{3}{5} = \square$

   d $\square \times \frac{4}{5} = 8$ therefore $8 \div \frac{4}{5} = \square$

22 Your answers to questions **15** and **21** will help you answer these.

   a When you multiply a positive number by a fraction less than one, is the
answer a smaller or larger number?

   b When you divide a positive number by a fraction less than one, is the
answer a smaller or larger number?

Percentages

- Calculating percentages of numbers, quantities and measurements
- Using percentages to solve problems
- Finding the outcome of a percentage increase or decrease

Keywords

You should know

explanation 1

1 Copy and complete the table.

	Fraction	Decimal	Percentage
a	$\frac{1}{4}$		
b		0.54	
c			16%
d	$\frac{1}{3}$		
e		0.625	
f			81%
g		0.98	

2 Write each percentage as a fraction in its lowest terms.

a	25%	b	24%	c	72%	d	62%
e	98%	f	45%	g	3%	h	12.5%

3 Write each decimal as a percentage.

a	0.69	b	0.12	c	0.05	d	0.39
e	0.485	f	0.027	g	1.64	h	3.51

4 Molly asked 60 pupils in her year to name their favourite flavour of crisp. Her results are in the table.

Plain	Cheese and onion	Salt and vinegar	BBQ	Prawn cocktail
4	15	8	21	12

a 21 out of the 60 pupils chose BBQ flavour.

This can be written as a fraction, $\frac{21}{60} = \frac{7}{20}$.

What fraction of the group chose each of the other flavours?

b What percentage of the group chose each flavour?

explanation 2a   explanation 2b

5 Work out each amount by first changing the percentage to a fraction.

    a 14% of 36   **b** 15% of 24   **c** 21% of 18   **d** 33% of 12

    e 35% of 40   **f** 48% of 9   **g** 75% of 42   **h** 8% of 96

    i 40% of 32   **j** 64% of 10   **k** 18% of 15   **l** 55% of 3

6 Find these amounts. If you use a calculator *do not* use the % key.

    a 37% of 84 kg   **b** 52% of 48 cm   **c** 18% of £72

    d 44% of 92 m   **e** 2.9% of 51 km   **f** 12.5% of 68 g

    g 32.6% of 28 m   **h** 18.7% of 55 km   **i** 120% of £32

    j 105% of 47 kg   **k** 2.5% of 576 cm   **l** 6.9% of £120

7 Work out each amount.

    a 46% of £95   **b** 24.5% of £70   **c** 35.5% of £52

    d 82.5% of £48   **e** 18% of £64   **f** 51.7% of £70

8 Peter puts £200 into a bank account which pays 4.5% interest a year. How much interest will he receive after one year?

9

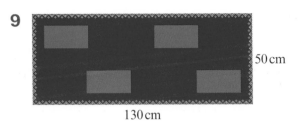

50 cm

130 cm

20% of this piece of fabric is green. What area of the fabric is green?

10

The pie chart shows how pupils in a class travel to school. 30 pupils travel by car.

a   How many pupils are in the class?

b   How many pupils walk to school?

explanation 3

11 Work out these percentages.

a   45 as a percentage of 60   b   15 as a percentage of 75

c   32 as a percentage of 128   d   42 as a percentage of 112

12 The human body consists of 206 bones.
There are 26 bones in each foot.
What percentage of the bones in
the human skeleton are in the feet?

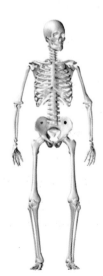

13 Peter receives £75 for his birthday. He saves
£50 and spends the rest on CDs.
What percentage did he save?

14 Steve's test scores are given in the table.

    a Copy and complete the table by working out Steve's percentage score for each subject.

Subject	Score	Percentage
English	$\frac{35}{40}$	
Maths	$\frac{68}{80}$	
Geography	$\frac{28}{35}$	
History	$\frac{54}{60}$	
Science	$\frac{56}{64}$	

    b In which subject did Steve achieve his best result?

15 Work out these percentages.

    a 40p as a percentage of £5

    b 18 minutes as a percentage of 4 hours

    c 30 g as a percentage of 1.5 kg

    d 63 cm as a percentage of 2.8 m

    e 15 mm as a percentage of 20 cm

    f 63 m as a percentage of 3 km

16 Sophie puts £250 into her savings account. After one year she receives £8.75 in interest. What was the rate of interest paid on her savings?

17 Kasia buys a sandwich and an apple for her lunch. The sandwich costs £1.20 and the apple costs 30p.

    a Find the cost of the sandwich as a percentage of the total cost of her lunch.

    b Find the cost of the apple as a percentage of the total cost of her lunch.

explanation 4

18 Each price is increased by the percentage shown. Calculate the new values.

   a   £30 is increased by 15%

   b   £65 is increased by 12%

   c   £82 is increased by 23%

   d   £16 is increased by 45%

   e   £124 is increased by 32%

19 The cost of electricity goes up by 11%. Find the new cost of electricity for each of these original costs.

   a   £70   b   £360   c   £470   d   £550

20 Council tax bills are increased by 4% this year.

   a   i Write this year's council tax bill as a percentage of last year's bill.

       ii Write the percentage in decimal form.

   b   How much will the council tax be this year if it was this much last year?

       i   £800   ii   £1050   iii   £1720

21 1640 people visited an art exhibition in September. The number of visitors in October was 5% higher. How many people visited the exhibition in October?

22 £2020 was raised at the school fair last year.

   a   This year the amount raised was 8% more than last year.
       How much money was raised this year?

   b   5% of the amount raised last year came from the ice cream stall.
       How much money did it take?

23 Martin and Susie bought a house for £150000 and a year later its value had increased by 4.5%. What was the value of their house after the increase?

> explanation 5

24 The following prices are reduced by the percentage shown. Calculate the new values.

    a £30 is reduced by 25%

    b £65 is reduced by 65%

    c £98 is reduced by 77%

    d £130 is reduced by 12%

    e £456 is reduced by 21%

25 A reduction of 5% is given if a customer buys gas and electricity from the same supplier. The total bill for gas and electricity is £784 before the discount is applied. How much will the customer actually pay?

26 Tom wants to buy a car which cost £5600. He can either pay the total in cash or pay a 20% deposit followed by 24 equal monthly payments of £190.

Tom buys the car using the second method.

    a How much is the deposit?

    b How much will Tom pay in instalments?

    c How much will he pay altogether?

    d How much more is this than if he paid cash?

27 House prices increase by 4% in June.
In November it is reported that house prices have fallen by 4%.
A house was valued at £240000 in May.
Work out the value of this house in December.

Mental methods (1)

• Using facts you know to answer unfamiliar questions

Keywords

You should know

You should answer the questions in this topic without using a calculator.

explanation 1

1 Write these fractions as decimals.

a $\dfrac{1}{5}$ b $\dfrac{3}{4}$ c $\dfrac{7}{20}$ d $\dfrac{6}{25}$

e $\dfrac{3}{8}$ f $\dfrac{4}{5}$ g $\dfrac{1}{3}$ h $\dfrac{9}{10}$

i $\dfrac{2}{3}$ j $\dfrac{1}{6}$ k $\dfrac{2}{5}$ l $\dfrac{7}{8}$

2 Use your answers to question **1** to write each fraction as a percentage.

3 Change these percentages to decimals.

a 13%   b 45%   c 5%   d 84%

e 36%   f 72%   g 12.5%   h 6.5%

4 Write each percentage in question **3** as a fraction. Give each answer in its simplest form.

explanation 2a   explanation 2b   explanation 2c

5 Calculate these percentages.

a 10% of 64   b 20% of 64   c 5% of 64   d 25% of 64

e 10% of 52   f 5% of 52   g 25% of 52   h 45% of 52

6 Work out the following percentages.

a   15% of £38   b   35% of 72 kg   c   21% of £62   d   43% of 56 litres

e   64% of 39 km   f   72% of 3 m   g   5% of 20 hours   h   3% of 15 g

7 The prices shown do not include VAT.

 £200    £550    £120

a   Work out the VAT, at a rate of 17.5%, for each item.

b   Find the total cost of each item, including VAT.

8 In a sale all items are reduced by 15%. For each item calculate these values.

    i The amount of the reduction   ii The sale price

a   trainers costing £45 before the sale

b   tennis racquet costing £38 before the sale

c   football costing £16 before the sale

d   hockey stick costing £55 before the sale

explanation 3

9 Copy and complete this table.

3	×	4	=	
2	×	4	=	
1	×	4	=	
0.1	×	4	=	
0.2	×	4	=	
0.3	×	4	=	

10 Use the fact that $8 \times 4 = 32$ to answer the following questions.

    a 8×0.4 **b** 0.8×4 **c** 0.8×0.4

    d 80×4 **e** 80×0.4 **f** 0.8×400

    g 80×40 **h** 8×0.04 **i** 80×0.04

11 Use the fact that $9 \times 7 = 63$ to answer these questions.

    a 0.9×7 **b** 0.9×0.7 **c** 9×0.7

    d 9×0.07 **e** 90×7 **f** 9×700

    g 0.09×7 **h** 90×0.7 **i** 0.09×700

12 Use the answer to the first division in each row to work out the other divisions in the row.

    a $20 \div 4$ **b** $2 \div 4$ **c** $0.2 \div 4$ **d** $0.02 \div 4$

    e $60 \div 5$ **f** $6 \div 5$ **g** $0.6 \div 5$ **h** $0.06 \div 5$

    i $18 \div 2$ **j** $1.8 \div 2$ **k** $0.18 \div 2$ **l** $0.018 \div 2$

    m $10 \div 4$ **n** $1 \div 4$ **o** $0.1 \div 4$ **p** $0.01 \div 4$

13 Copy and complete.

    a $0.2 \times \square = 6$ **b** $4 \times \square = 0.8$

    c $0.1 \times \square = 0.4$ **d** $3 \div \square = 3$

    e $\square \div 5 = 0.2$ **f** $10 \div \square = 0.5$

14 Make 36 using the digits 1, 3 , 3 and 5 once, together with any combination of the symbols $+, -, \times, \div$ and brackets.

15 Andy was born in 1982. Using the digits of that year, in any order, together with any combination of the symbols $+, -, \times, \div$ and brackets, how many numbers between 1 and 30 can you make?

Simplifying expressions

- Identifying the correct order for calculations involving algebra
- Simplifying expressions by collecting like terms
- Expanding simple expressions involving brackets
- Writing expressions using index notation

Keywords

You should know

explanation 1a   explanation 1b   explanation 1c

1 Work these out.

a $\dfrac{4+6}{2}$

b $\dfrac{4}{2}+6$

c $4+\dfrac{6}{2}$

d $\dfrac{9-6}{3}$

e $\dfrac{9}{3}-6$

f $9-\dfrac{6}{3}$

2 Work these out.

a $2+3^2$

b 2^2+3^2

c $2(2+3)$

3 Which of these expressions is equivalent to $\dfrac{p+q}{r}$?

a $p \div r + q$

b $(p+q) \div r$

c $p + q \div r$

4 Look at these expressions. In what order are the operations carried out?

a $p+3q$

b p^2-11

c $2-\dfrac{q}{p}$

d $4(p+q^2)$

explanation 2a   explanation 2b   explanation 2c

5 Simplify these expressions. Collect like terms.

a $y+2y$

b $2x+4x+x$

c $3p+q+2p$

d $c+2d+4c-d$

e $6y-3z-8y+4z$

f $8m-2j+6m-3m-4j$

g $3s+6t+u+s-u-8t$

h $x+y+y-x-z+z$

i $3+a+4a$

j $5+3p+2p$

k $-4+m-2m+6$

l $-3+2a+2b+a-3-2b$

6 Write an expression for the perimeter of each shape. Simplify your answers.

a

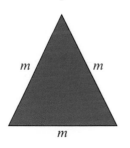

m m

m

b

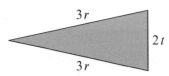

$3r$

$2t$

$3r$

c

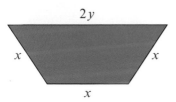

$2y$

x x

x

d

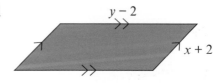

$y - 2$

$x + 2$

e

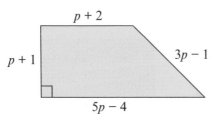

$p + 2$

$p + 1$ $3p - 1$

$5p - 4$

f

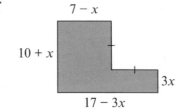

$7 - x$

$10 + x$

$3x$

$17 - 3x$

explanation 3a   explanation 3b

7 Expand each expression.

  a $2(x + 1)$ **b** $3(5 + y)$ **c** $5(p + q)$

  d $6(4a + 3)$ **e** $4(y - 2z)$ **f** $3(t - 3q)$

  g $5(2m + 3n)$ **h** $6(3a - 2b)$ **i** $-4(2x - 4y)$

  j $a(2 + b)$ **k** $p(4 - q)$ **l** $x(y + z)$

  m $2m(2 + n)$ **n** $3g(2 + g)$ **o** $4p(p - 2q)$

8 Expand the brackets and simplify the expressions.

  a $3m(a + 2) + 2m$ **b** $5x(y + 3) + 2xy - 1$

  c $5a(x + y) + 2ax + ay$ **d** $\frac{1}{2}a(4m - 2n) + an$

  e $k(p + q) + k(3p - q)$ **f** $5c(d + 2e) + 2c(3d + e)$

  g $4p(2q - r) - 2p(q + r)$ **h** $x(y - z) - x(y + z)$

9 Write an expression for the area of each rectangle. Expand the brackets.

a
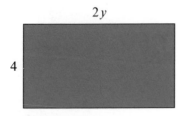

b
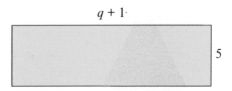

c
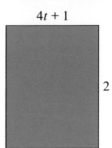

d
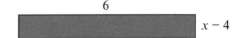

10 What is the area of the shaded part of the rectangle?

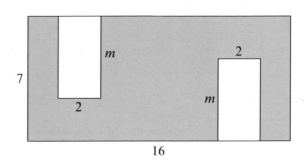

explanation 4a   explanation 4b

11 Write these using index notation.

    a $y \times y \times y$ **b** $r \times r \times r \times r$ **c** $p \times p \times p \times p \times p$

    d $t \times t \times u \times u \times u$ **e** $y \times y \times y \times z$ **f** $a \times a \times b \times b \times c \times c$

    g $m \times n \times n \times p \times p \times p$ **h** $d \times d \times d \times d \times e \times e$ **i** $s \times s \times t \times s$

12 Write these in full.

    a t^2 **b** $f^2 g$ **c** $b^3 d^2$ **d** $y^4 z^3$ **e** $a^2 b^2 c^3$ **f** $mn^3 p^2$

13 **a** Write each of these expressions in full.

       i $a^4 \times b \times a$ **ii** $x \times y^2 \times x^3$ **iii** $p^3 \times q \times p \times q^2$

    b Write each expression in part **a** as simply as possible using index notation.

Using equations

- Forming and solving simple equations

explanation 1a explanation 1b explanation 1c

1 Solve these equations.

a $x + 2 = 6$

b $t - 3 = 7$

c $3 + m = 2$

d $3x - 2 = 16$

e $8 = 12a - 4$

f $22 = 6b - 8$

g $12 + 4p = 4$

h $6a + 1 = -5$

i $5d - 4 = -19$

explanation 2a explanation 2b explanation 2c

2 Solve these equations.

a $12x = 2x + 10$

b $7x - 8 = 3x$

c $6a + 3 = 2a + 7$

d $9p - 4 = 10p - 5$

e $4q + 6 = 3q + 2$

f $6 - n = n - 4$

g $3 - 4n = 2n - 15$

h $7n - 20 = -3n$

i $4f + 3 = 8 - f$

j $2 + 7t = t + 11$

k $-r - 5 = 4 + 2r$

l $4 - 7s = 3s + 4$

3 Solve these equations.

a $2(x + 1) = 6$

b $5(m - 2) = 15$

c $5 = 2(a - 1)$

d $4(p - 6) = 0$

e $3(y + 6) - 24 = 0$

f $2(z + 1) + 3 = 5$

g $\dfrac{x + 1}{2} = 3$

h $\dfrac{8}{b} = 4$

i $5 + \dfrac{8}{c} = 21$

j $4 - \dfrac{9}{k} = 7$

k $\dfrac{3}{p} + 4 = 0$

l $\dfrac{25}{g} = g$

4 Solve these equations.

Expand brackets first, then eliminate the letter from one side of the equation.

a $2(2x + 3) = 3(x + 1)$

b $6(3g + 2) = 4(4g + 7)$

c $3(m + 1) + 2(2m + 9) = 0$

d $2(3f + 5) - 12 = 16$

5 What is the size of each angle in these triangles? Write equations and solve them.

a

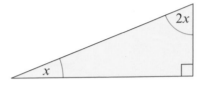

b

c

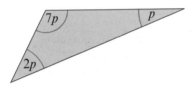

d

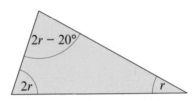

6 What is the size of each angle in these quadrilaterals? Write equations and solve them.

Remember
The sum of angles in
a quadrilateral is 360°.

a

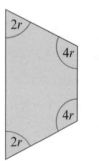

b

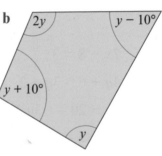

c

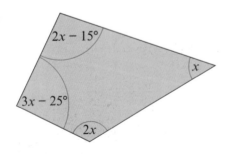

d

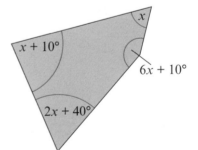

7 Write an equation for the perimeter of each rectangle. Use your equations to help you to work out the width and length of each rectangle.

a Perimeter = 36 cm

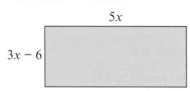

b Perimeter = 110 cm

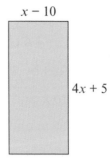

c Perimeter = 50 cm

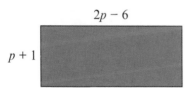

d Perimeter = 46 cm

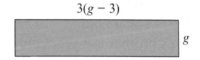

8 Write an equation for the perimeter of each shape.
Use your equations to help you to work out the length of each side.

a Perimeter = 56 cm

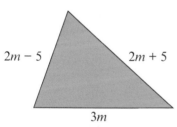

b Perimeter = 74 cm

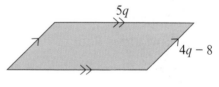

c Perimeter = 36 cm

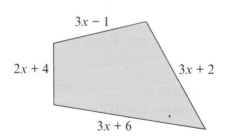

d Perimeter = 40 cm

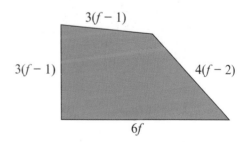

explanation 4a   explanation 4b

9 What is the value of each letter? Write and solve equations to help you.

  a When x is doubled and 4 added, the result is 12.

  b When y is trebled and 6 subtracted, the result is 6.

  c When p is multiplied by 4 and 3 added, the result is 27.

  d When 2 is added to k and the answer multiplied by 5, the result is 25.

  e When 4 is added to m and the answer multiplied by 6, the result is 24.

  f When 3 is subtracted from twice q and the answer multiplied by 3, the result is 27.

10 Paula is y years old.
Paula's brother is 7 years older than Paula.
Paula's sister is 2 years younger than Paula.

  a Write an expression in terms of y for the sum of the ages of the three children.

  b The sum of the ages of the three children is 20.
  Use your answer to part **a** to write an equation involving y.

  c How old is Paula?

  d How old are Paula's brother and sister?

11 On Tuesday, Kate spent x minutes on her homework.

Ibrahim spent 20 minutes more than Kate.

Miguel spent 20 minutes more than Ibrahim.

  a Write an expression in terms of x for the total time Kate, Ibrahim and Miguel spent on their homework.

  b Kate, Ibrahim and Miguel spent a total of 120 minutes on their homework. Use your answer to part **a** to write an equation involving x.

  c How long did Kate spend on her homework?

  d How long did Ibrahim and Miguel spend on their homework?

12 Three houses are for sale.

Acacia House is on sale for £*x*.

Beech Hall is on sale for twice as much as Acacia House.

Chestnut Cottage is on sale for £100 000 more than Acacia House.

The total sale price of the three houses is £600 000.

Acacia House   Beech Hall   Chestnut Cottage

  a   Write an equation in terms of *x* for the total sale price of the three houses.

  b   What is the sale price of Acacia House?

  c   What is the sale price of Beech Hall and Chestnut Cottage?

13 Two barrels P and Q contain 11 litres and 3 litres of water respectively.

x litres of water is added to both barrels.

  a   Write expressions in terms of *x* for the amount of water in each barrel after the extra water is added.

Barrel P now has three times the amount of water as barrel Q.

  b   Write an equation in terms of *x* in order to show the relationship between the amounts of water in the barrels.

  c   What is the amount of water added to each barrel?

  d   What is the amount of water in both barrels after the water is added?

Algebra A2.3

Formulae

- Substituting values into expressions and formulae
- Deriving simple formulae

Keywords

You should know

---

explanation 1a   explanation 1b

1 $p = 2$, $q = 3$ and $r = -4$. Find the value of s for each formula.

   a $s = 2p + q$
   b $s = 2p + 3q$
   c $s = 3q - r$

   d $s = p + q + 2r$
   e $s = 4r - 3q + p$
   f $s = 2(q + r)$

   g $s = 4(2q - r)$
   h $s = 5(2p - q)$
   i $s = 4(3p - 2q)$

   j $s = \dfrac{4}{q}$
   k $s = \dfrac{2p + q}{r}$
   l $s = \dfrac{r + 1}{r - 1}$

---

explanation 2

2 $x = 2$, $y = 3$ and $z = 5$. Find the value of w for each formula.

   a $w = y^2 + x$
   b $w = y + z^2$
   c $w = x^3 + y^2$

   d $w = 2y^2 + z$
   e $w = 3x^2 - 2y$
   f $w = z^2 - 2x^3$

   g $w = 2z^2 + y^2$
   h $w = x^2 + y^2 + z^2$
   i $w = x^3 - y^2 - z$

3 The cost (C pence) of hiring a minicab is given by the formula $C = 200 + 25d$, where d is the number of kilometres travelled.
Calculate C for these values of d.

   a $d = 5$
   b $d = 10$
   c $d = 20$

4 The cost (P pounds) of calling out an emergency plumber is given by the formula $P = 60 + 40t$, where t is the number of hours the job takes to complete.
Calculate P for these values of t.

   a $t = 1$
   b $t = 3$
   c $t = 8$

5 Zoe and Tim investigated how long it took pupils to get to school. They found that the time taken (T minutes) could be approximately calculated using the formula $T = 15a + 3b$.

a is the distance in kilometres from their home to the bus stop and b is the distance in kilometres from the bus stop to the school.

Calculate T for these values of a and b.

  a $a = 1, b = 6$ **b** $a = 2, b = 4$ **c** $a = 3, b = 12$

6 The velocity of a car can be calculated using the formula $v = u + at$.
v is the final velocity of the car in metres per second.
u is the initial velocity of the car in metres per second.
a is the acceleration of the car in metres per second per second.
t is the time spent accelerating in seconds.

Calculate v for these values of u, a, and t.

  a $u = 5, a = 1, t = 5$ **b** $u = 6, a = 2, t = 3$ **c** $u = 0, a = 2, t = 10$

7 The area of a triangle is given by the formula $A = \frac{1}{2}bh$, where b is the length of the base of the triangle and h is its height.

Calculate the area of the triangle for these values of b and h.

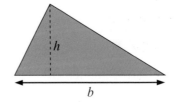

  a $b = 6\,\text{cm}, h = 3\,\text{cm}$

  b $b = 12\,\text{cm}, h = 5\,\text{cm}$

  c $b = 1\,\text{cm}, h = 8\,\text{cm}$

  d $b = 7\,\text{cm}, h = 4\,\text{cm}$

8 The volume of a rectangular-based pyramid is given by the formula $V = \frac{1}{3}lwh$, where l is the length of the base, w is the width of the base and h is the height of the pyramid.

Calculate the volume of the pyramid for these values of l, w and h.

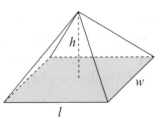

  a $l = 2\,\text{cm}, w = 3\,\text{cm}, h = 5\,\text{cm}$

  b $l = 6\,\text{cm}, w = 5\,\text{cm}, h = 2\,\text{cm}$

  c $l = 6\,\text{cm}, w = 8\,\text{cm}, h = 4\,\text{cm}$

explanation 3

9 A piece of string is 20 cm long. A piece of length x cm is cut from it.

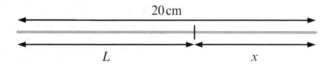

    a Write a formula for calculating the length, L cm, of the string that is left.

    b Calculate L when $x = 6$ cm.

    c Calculate x when $L = 18$ cm.

> Write a formula for calculating the length, x cm, that is cut off.

10 A plank of length L cm is cut into three sections, x cm, y cm and z cm long.

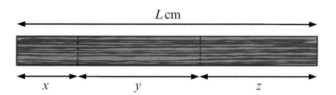

    a Write a formula for the length x in terms of L, y, and z.

    b The total length, L cm, of the plank is 120 cm.

       i Calculate x when $y = 50$ and $z = 30$.

      ii Calculate y when $x = 40$ and $z = 75$.

     iii Calculate z when $x = 32$ and $y = 56$.

11 A rectangle has length l cm and width w cm. Its area is A cm^2.

    a Write a formula for the area of the rectangle.

    b Calculate A when $l = 6$ and $w = 8$.

    c Calculate A when $l = 9$ and $w = 7$.

l

w   Area A

12 A rectangle has length a cm and width b cm.

    a Write a formula for the perimeter (P cm) of the rectangle.

    b Calculate P when $a = 3$ and $b = 4$.

    c Calculate P when $a = 6$ and $b = 5$.

    d Calculate a when $P = 20$ and $b = 1$.

    e Calculate b when $P = 52$ and $a = 11$.

> Write formulae for calculating a and b.

Area

- Calculating the area of triangles, parallelograms and trapeziums
- Calculating the area of compound shapes

Keywords

You should know

explanation 1a   explanation 1b

1 Calculate the area of these triangles.

a

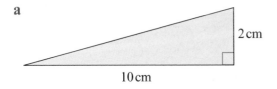

2 cm

10 cm

b

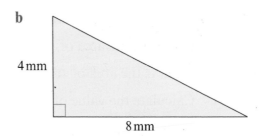

4 mm

8 mm

c

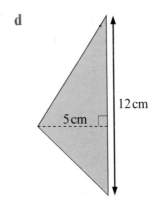

5 m

4 m

10 m

d

12 cm

5 cm

e

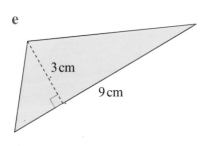

3 cm

9 cm

f

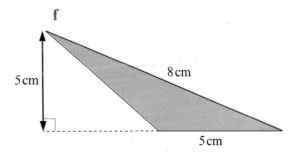

5 cm

8 cm

5 cm

2 Calculate the height of each triangle. (The area and the base length of each triangle is given.)

    a Area $= 25\,\text{cm}^2$

    b Area $= 20\,\text{mm}^2$

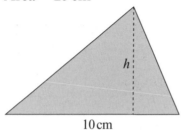
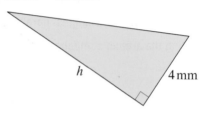

3 Triangle B has double the area of triangle A.

    The height of both triangles is 6 cm.

    a Calculate the area of triangle A.

    b What is the area of triangle B?

    c Calculate the value of x.

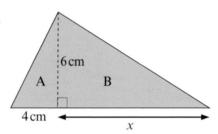

4 The area of triangle Y is three times that of triangle X.

    a Calculate the area of triangle X.

    b Calculate the area of triangle Y.

    c Calculate the height of triangle Y.

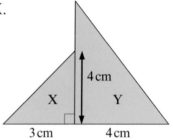

5 Look at this diagram.

    a Calculate the area of triangle ABE.

    b Calculate the area of triangle ACD.

    c Calculate the area of the trapezium BCDE.

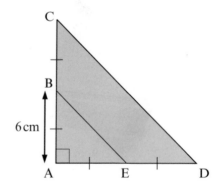

explanation 2a   explanation 2b

6 Calculate the area of these parallelograms.

a
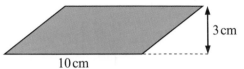
3 cm
10 cm

b
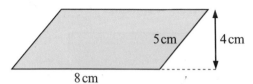
5 cm
4 cm
8 cm

c

8 cm
4 cm

d
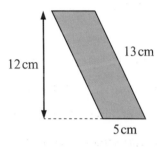
13 cm
12 cm
5 cm

e
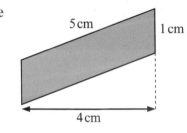
5 cm
1 cm
4 cm

f
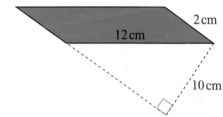
2 cm
12 cm
10 cm

explanation 3a   explanation 3b

7 Calculate the area of these trapeziums.

a
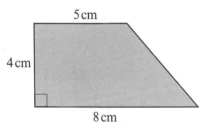
5 cm
4 cm
8 cm

b
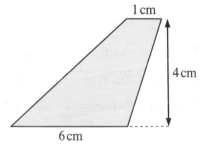
1 cm
4 cm
6 cm

c
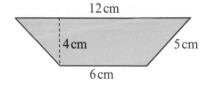
12 cm
4 cm
5 cm
6 cm

d
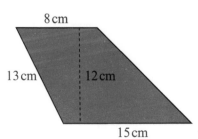
8 cm
13 cm
12 cm
15 cm

explanation 4a   explanation 4b

8 Calculate the marked lengths in these shapes.

a Area = 100 cm²

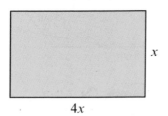

b Area = 51 cm²

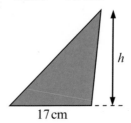

c Area = 150 cm²

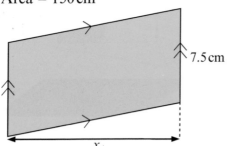

d Area = 96 cm²

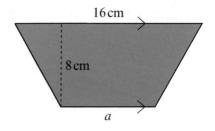

explanation 5

9 Calculate the area of these compound shapes.

a

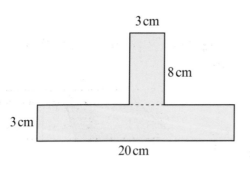

b

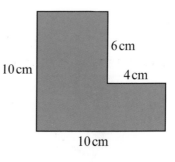

c

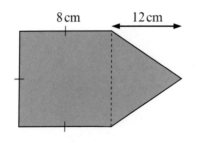

d

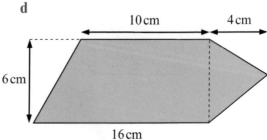

10 Calculate the shaded area of each of these.

a

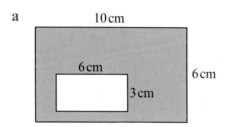

b

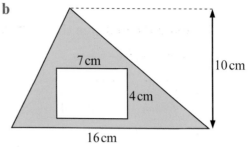

c

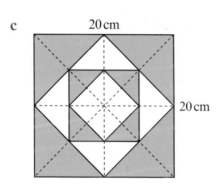

d

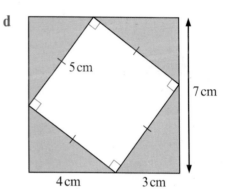

11 An arrowhead has dimensions as shown.

Showing your method clearly, calculate the shaded area.

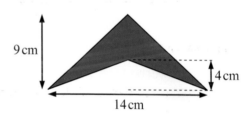

12 The side of a house has the dimensions shown. Showing your method clearly, calculate the area of this side of the house.

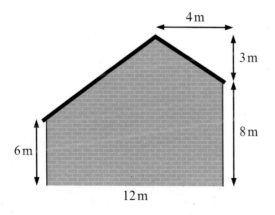

Hint: can you divide the shape into two trapeziums?

13 These questions are about compound shapes made from rectangles, triangles and trapeziums.

    a Calculate the area that is shaded.

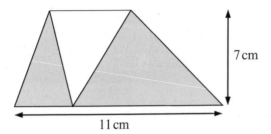

    b A piece of guttering has a cross-section as shown.

       Calculate the area of the cross-section.

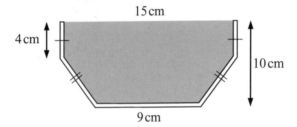

    c A garden consists of a rectangular patch of grass, C, and two triangular flowerbeds, A and B.

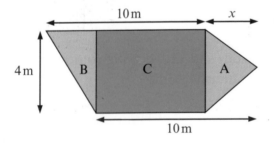

       i Write an expression for the area of A.

       ii Write an expression for the area of B.

       iii Write an expression for the area of C.

       iv Work out the total area of the garden.

Geometry and measures GM2.2

Volume

- Calculating the volume of cuboids and of shapes made of cuboids
- Calculating the surface area of cuboids and shapes made from cuboids

Keywords

You should know

explanation 1a   explanation 1b   explanation 1c   explanation 1d

1 Calculate the volume of these cuboids.

a

3 cm
2 cm
8 cm

b

1 cm
9.5 cm

c

1 m
9 m
6 m

d

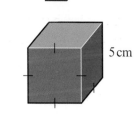

5 cm

2 Calculate the total surface area of each of the cuboids in question **1**.

3 a A cube has edge length 10 mm.
What is its volume in cubic millimetres (mm^3)?

b What is the volume of a cube of edge length 1 cm, in cubic centimetres (cm^3)?

c Ahmed has measured the volume of some containers in cubic centimetres.
What simple rule can he use to convert his measurements into cubic millimetres?

Use your answers to parts **a** and **b**.

4 The volumes of these cuboids are given.

Calculate the lengths of the sides marked by letters.

a Volume = 96 cm³

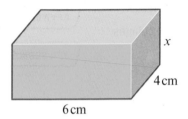

6 cm, 4 cm, x

b Volume = 128 cm³

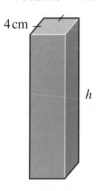

4 cm, h

c Volume = 100 cm³

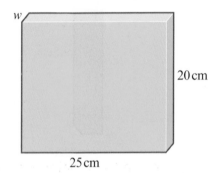

w, 20 cm, 25 cm

d Volume = 343 cm³

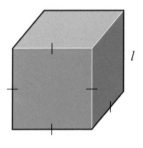

l

5 Two cuboids are stuck together to make this shape.

a Calculate the volume of the shape.

b What is the area of face A?

c Calculate the surface area of faces B, C, D and E.

d What is the total surface area of the shape?

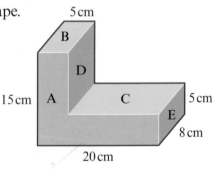

5 cm, B, D, 15 cm, A, C, E, 5 cm, 8 cm, 20 cm

6 Two cuboids are stuck together to make this shape.

a Calculate the volume of the shape.

b Calculate the total surface area.

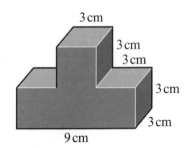

3 cm, 3 cm, 3 cm, 3 cm, 3 cm, 9 cm

7 Three cuboids are stuck together to make this shape.

   a Calculate the volume of the shape.

   b Calculate the total surface area.

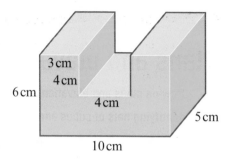

8 A cube of edge length 2 cm is placed on top of a cuboid.

   a What is the volume of the combined shape?

   b Calculate the total surface area of the shape.

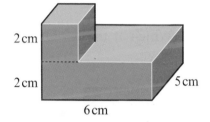

9 Cube A has edge length 2 cm.
   The edges of cube B are twice as long as those of cube A.

   a Calculate the volume of cube A.

   b What is the total surface area of cube A?

   c How many times bigger is the volume of B compared to the volume of A?

   d How many times bigger is the surface area of B compared to the surface area of A?

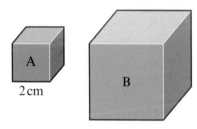

Plans and elevations

- Drawing plans and elevations of 3–D shapes
- Identifying nets of cubes and cuboids

Keywords

You should know

explanation 1

1 Which of these 3-D shapes are prisms?

> A prism has the same cross-section at any point along its length.

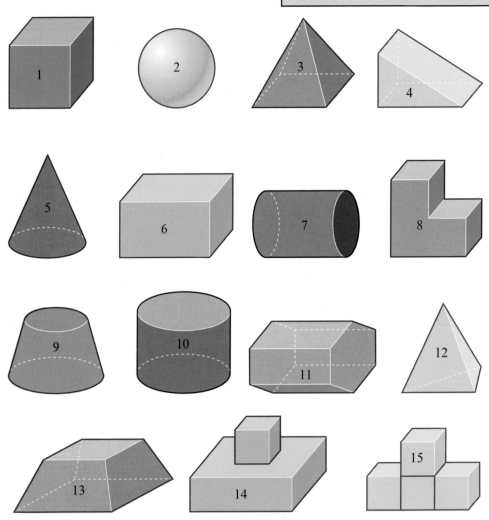

2 Which of the 3-D shapes in question **1** match to each plan below?

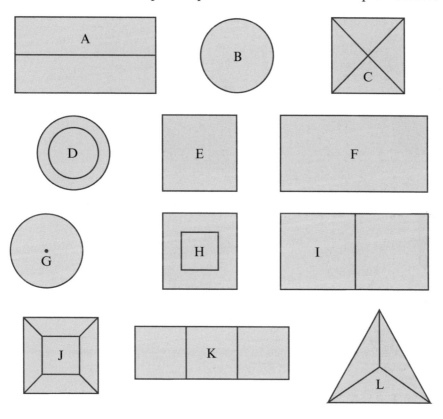

3 Which of the 3-D shapes for question **1** match to each side elevation below? Each elevation shows the shape as seen from the right.

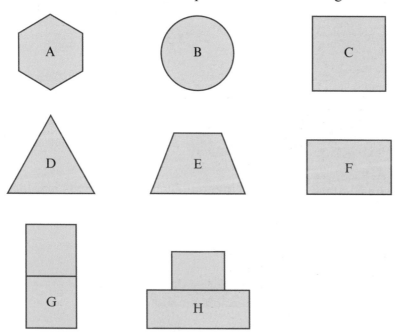

4 Each diagram shows a 3-D shape made from cubes.

  i Draw a plan of each shape.

  ii Draw a side elevation of each shape, as seen from the left.

a

b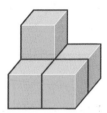

c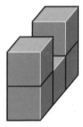

d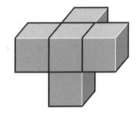

(explanation 2a)   (explanation 2b)   (explanation 2c) ———————————————

4 Which of these are nets of a cube?

A
	1	
2	3	4
	5	
	6	

B
3	2	1
4		
5		
6		

C
2	1
3	
4	
5	6

D
		2
	1	3
5	4	
6		

E
5			
4	1	2	3
6			

F
1			
2	3	4	5
			6

G
	5		
1	2	3	4
		6	

5 Look at your answers to question 4. Imagine that each of those nets is folded to make a cube. For each net, which face would be opposite face 1 when folded?

6 Draw two nets for this cuboid.

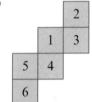

1 cm

2 cm

4 cm

Units of measurement

- Making rough conversions between metric and imperial measures
- Justifying an appropriate degree of accuracy for a measurement

Keywords

You should know

explanation 1a explanation 1b explanation 1c

1 Copy and complete each statement.

a $8\,\text{km} = \square\,\text{m}$

b $1500\,\text{m} = \square\,\text{km}$

c $8.5\,\text{m} = \square\,\text{cm}$

d $70\,\text{cm} = \square\,\text{mm}$

e $0.65\,\text{m} = \square\,\text{mm}$

f $560\,\text{cm} = \square\,\text{km}$

g $2\text{ hectares} = \square\,\text{m}^2$

h $5400\,\text{cm}^2 = \square\,\text{m}^2$

i $875\,\text{g} = \square\,\text{kg}$

j $1.305\,\text{kg} = \square\,\text{g}$

k $3.5\text{ litres} = \square\,\text{cm}^3$

l $950\text{ litres} = \square\,\text{m}^3$

2 Copy and complete the table. Choose from the items shown.
One has been done for you.

	Approximate measure	Type of measure	Item
	2 m	length	door
a	1 tonne		
b	750 ml		
c	7500 m²		
d	100 g		
e	10 m		
f	480 mm²		
g	200 litres		
h	1 kg		
i	50 cm²		
j	15 cm		

3 On average, a person lives for about 40 000 000 minutes.

    a Work out how long this is to the nearest

       i hour

      ii day

     iii year

> In part **a iii**, assume that every year has 365 days.

    b How many leap years are there in an average lifetime?
Give your answer to the nearest whole number.

> Hint: about one in every four years is a leap year. 'One in four' is the same as one quarter

4 Justin has 547 tracks on his music player.

On average, each track is about $3\frac{1}{2}$ minutes long.

How long would they take to play altogether in days and hours, to the nearest hour?

5 A fish tank is in the shape of a cuboid.
It can hold a maximum of 27 litres.
The base of the tank is made of plastic.
It is 25 cm wide and 50 cm long.

    a What is the height of the fish tank?

    b What is the area of glass needed to make the four sides of the tank?

6 Anthony is writing to his pen pal who lives in Paris.

    a Anthony says that the distance from Manchester to Paris is 600 km.
What do you think this measurement is correct to?

       To the nearest 10 metres   To the nearest 100 metres

       To the nearest kilometre   To the nearest 10 kilometres

    b Anthony says that the flight from Manchester to Paris takes 1.5 hours.
What do you think this measurement is correct to?

       To the nearest second   To the nearest 10 seconds

       To the nearest minute   To the nearest 10 minutes

       To the nearest hour

explanation 2a   explanation 2b   explanation 2c

7 Approximately how many gallons will
these fuel tanks hold?
Give your answers to the nearest gallon.

a 55 litres

b 75 litres

c 80 litres

8 a Convert these amounts to pounds. Write your answers to the nearest 0.1 lb.

    i 1 kg   **ii** 1.5 kg   **iii** 500 g

b Convert these amounts to kilograms. Write your answers to the nearest 0.1 kg.

    i 2 lb   **ii** $5\frac{1}{2}$ lb

c Sharon is going shopping. This is her shopping list.

Work out how much each item would cost to the
nearest penny at

    i Greene's Grocers   **ii** Mason's Fruit & Veg

d Sharon wants to do all her shopping at one shop.

Which shop should she choose if she wants to pay as little as possible?

> 1 kg bananas
> 2 lb mushrooms
> 500 g grapes
> 1.5 kg apples
> $5\frac{1}{2}$ lb potatoes

9 In an athletics competition, Rosa runs in both the mile and the 1500 metres
races. Which race is longer and by how far?
Give your answer to the nearest 10 metres.

Functions

- Writing a function machine as an equation
- Identifying and writing more complex rules linking inputs and outputs

Keywords

You should know

explanation 1a   explanation 1b

1 Write each function machine as an equation.

a $x \rightarrow \boxed{\times 2} \rightarrow y$

b $x \rightarrow \boxed{+ 5} \rightarrow y$

c $x \rightarrow \boxed{- 6} \rightarrow y$

d $x \rightarrow \boxed{\times 2} \rightarrow \boxed{+ 1} \rightarrow y$

e $q \rightarrow \boxed{\times 3} \rightarrow \boxed{- 1} \rightarrow p$

f $t \rightarrow \boxed{\times 5} \rightarrow \boxed{- 4} \rightarrow y$

g $b \rightarrow \boxed{\times 4} \rightarrow \boxed{+ 1} \rightarrow a$

h $k \rightarrow \boxed{\times 2} \rightarrow \boxed{+ 5} \rightarrow j$

i $x \rightarrow \boxed{\div 2} \rightarrow y$

j $x \rightarrow \boxed{\div 2} \rightarrow \boxed{+ 2} \rightarrow y$

k $d \rightarrow \boxed{\div 3} \rightarrow \boxed{- 4} \rightarrow c$

l $g \rightarrow \boxed{\div 2} \rightarrow \boxed{\times 2} \rightarrow f$

2 What is the rule that links each set of input and output numbers?

    i Write each rule as a function machine.

    ii Write each rule as an equation.

a

Input (x)	Output (y)
1	4
2	5
3	6
4	7
5	8

b

Input (x)	Output (y)
1	3
2	6
3	9
4	12
5	15

c

Input (x)	Output (y)
1	$\frac{1}{2}$
2	1
3	$1\frac{1}{2}$
4	2
5	$2\frac{1}{2}$

explanation 2a   explanation 2b

3 Write an equation for each function machine. Simplify where possible.

a $x \rightarrow \boxed{+2} \rightarrow \boxed{-7} \rightarrow y$

b $a \rightarrow \boxed{\div 3} \rightarrow \boxed{\times 6} \rightarrow b$

c $d \rightarrow \boxed{-3} \rightarrow \boxed{+4} \rightarrow c$

d $g \rightarrow \boxed{\div 2} \rightarrow \boxed{\times 2} \rightarrow f$

e $x \rightarrow \boxed{\div 2} \rightarrow \boxed{\times 4} \rightarrow y$

f $x \rightarrow \boxed{\div 4} \rightarrow \boxed{\times 2} \rightarrow y$

4 Use algebra to write the rule for each set of input and output numbers.
Write each rule

    i in the form $x \rightarrow \square$

    ii in the form $y = \square$

a

Input (x)	Output (y)
1	0
2	2
3	4
4	6
5	8

b

Input (x)	Output (y)
1	5
2	9
3	13
4	17
5	21

c

Input (x)	Output (y)
1	6
2	9
3	12
4	15
5	18

d

Input (x)	Output (y)
1	0
2	3
3	6
4	9
5	12

e

Input (x)	Output (y)
1	1
2	1.5
3	2
4	2.5
5	3

f

Input (x)	Output (y)
1	$\frac{3}{4}$
2	$\frac{3}{2}$
3	$2\frac{1}{4}$
4	3
5	$3\frac{3}{4}$

Functions and mappings

● Constructing a mapping diagram from a function machine

Keywords

You should know

explanation 1

1 In these questions mappings are given using algebra.

    i Write each mapping as a function machine.

    ii Copy and complete each table and mapping diagram.

a **i** $x \rightarrow x + 3$

    ii

Input	Output
1	4
2	5
3	
4	
5	

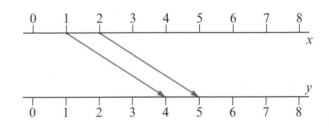

b **i** $x \rightarrow x - 2$

    ii

Input	Output
1	−1
2	
3	
4	
5	

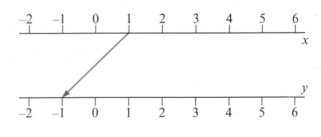

2 For each mapping below:

    i write the mapping as a function machine.

    ii copy and complete the table and mapping diagram.

a   **i** $x \rightarrow 2x$

    ii

Input	Output
0	
1	
2	
3	6
4	

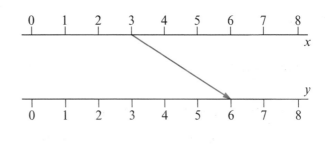

b   **i** $x \rightarrow 2x - 2$

    ii

Input	Output
1	
2	2
3	
4	
5	

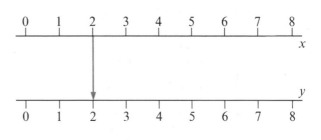

3 What do you notice about the lines in your mappings for questions **1** and **2**?

4 For each of the mappings below:

    i write the mapping as a function machine

    ii draw a table of inputs and outputs for input values 1, 2, 3, 4, and 5

    iii draw a mapping diagram

a $x \rightarrow -x$ **b** $x \rightarrow -x + 2$ **c** $x \rightarrow -2x$ **d** $x \rightarrow -2x + 3$

Functions and graphs

- Describing a straight line using an equation
- Writing an equation for a straight line in the form $y = mx + c$

Keywords

You should know

explanation 1

1 For each graph, copy and complete the table. The tables show the coordinates of the points marked with crosses.

a

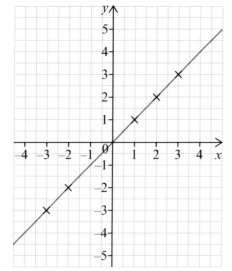

x	y
−3	
−2	
1	
2	
3	

b

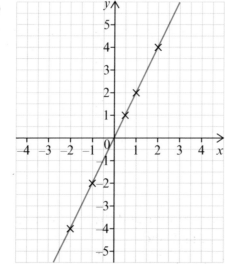

x	y
−2	
−1	
$\frac{1}{2}$	
1	
2	

2 Draw a table like this for each of the graphs below.

In each table, write the coordinates of the points marked on the line.

x	y

a
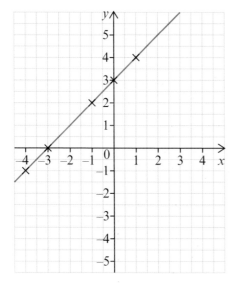

b
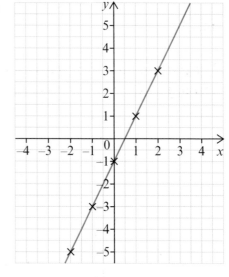

c
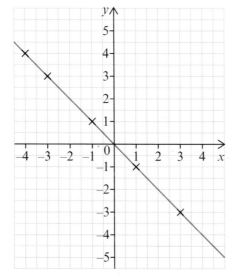

d
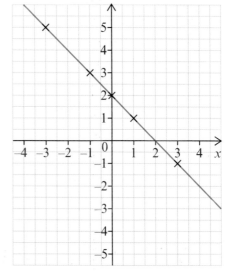

3 Look at the graphs in questions **1** and **2**.

  i In words, write the rule that links the x-coordinate and the y-coordinate of each point in each of the graphs in questions **1** and **2**.

  ii Write an equation for each rule in the form $y = \square$.

4 Copy and complete the table for each of these equations of straight lines.

x	y
-2	
-1	
0	
1	
2	

a $y = x + 2$ **b** $y = x - 4$

c $y = 2x + 1$ **d** $y = 2x - 2$

e $y = 3x$ **f** $y = -x + 1$

g $y = -2x + 3$ **h** $y = \frac{1}{2}x$

i $y = \frac{1}{2}x - 3$ **j** $y = -\frac{1}{2}x + 1$

5 Using each of your tables of coordinates from question **4**, plot the points on a pair of axes.

Draw a straight line through the points.

6 Some of the lines you drew in question **5** are parallel to each other.

  a Write down the equations of all the pairs of parallel lines.

  b What do the equations of parallel lines have in common?

explanation 2

7 Write the equation of each of the straight lines in the diagram.

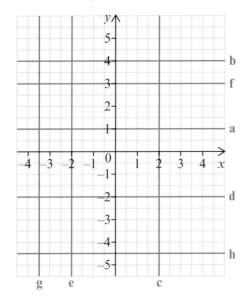

explanation 3a   explanation 3b

8 Which line do you think matches which equation? The line $y = x$ is labelled.

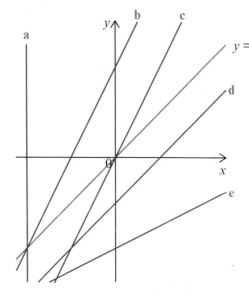

$y = 2x + 4$

$x = -3$

$y = x - 2$

$y = 2x$

$y = \frac{1}{2}x - 4$

9 Which line do you think matches which equation? The line $y = x$ is labelled.

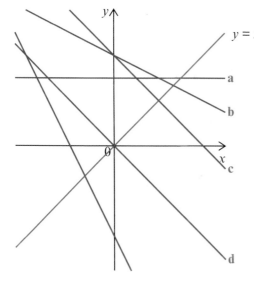

$y = -x$

$y = -2x - 4$

$y = -\frac{1}{2}x + 4$

$y = 3$

$y = -x + 4$

Place value, ordering and rounding

- Multiplying and dividing integers and decimals by 0.1 and 0.01
- Rounding numbers to the nearest multiple of a given power of 10
- Rounding numbers to either 1 or 2 decimal places
- Rounding decimals to the nearest whole number

Keywords

You should know

explanation 1

1 Write these numbers as multiples of 10. The first one has been done for you.

a $10^2 = 10 \times 10$
b 10^3
c 10^1
d 10^7
e $10^2 \times 10^1$
f $10^3 \times 10^2$

2 Write these as numbers.

a 2×10^2
b 4×10^3
c 9×10^4
d 7×10^5
e 8×10^6
f 2.1×10^2
g 3.5×10^3
h 1.25×10^2

3 Write these numbers using powers of 10.

a six hundred
b five thousand
c eighty thousand
d ten
e twelve thousand
f twenty hundred
g one hundred thousand
h three billion
i two hundred million

explanation 2a   explanation 2b

4 Without a calculator, work out these multiplications.

a 23×0.1
b 99×0.1
c 149×0.1
d 8×0.1
e 765×0.01
f 55×0.01
g 9×0.01
h $6581 \times 0.1 \times 0.01$
i $62 \times 0.01 \times 0.1$

5 Without a calculator, work out these divisions.

    a $3 \div 0.1$ **b** $20 \div 0.1$ **c** $169 \div 0.1$

    d $100 \div 0.1$ **e** $2 \div 0.01$ **f** $14 \div 0.01$

    g $128 \div 0.01$ **h** $5 \div 0.1 \div 0.01$ **i** $85 \div 0.01 \div 0.1$

> explanation 3

6 Write a multiplication and its answer for each diagram. The length of the side of each small square is 0.1 of the length of the large square.

a

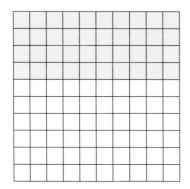

b

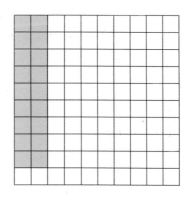

c

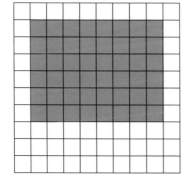

d

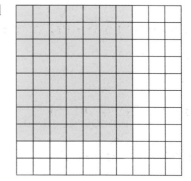

7 Write a division and its answer for each diagram in question **6**.

8 Without a calculator, work out these calculations.

    a 0.3×0.2 **b** 0.8×0.4 **c** 0.5×0.9

    d $0.6 \div 0.3$ **e** $0.6 \div 0.2$ **f** $0.9 \div 0.1$

9 Without a calculator, work out these calculations.

a 1.2×0.1 b 2.4×0.2 c 1.5×0.01

d $2.5 \div 0.1$ e $3.6 \div 0.01$ f $4.8 \div 0.2$

10 Find the missing number in each calculation.

a $0.4 \times 0.1 = \square$ b $0.2 \times 0.01 = \square$ c $0.8 \times \square = 0.24$

d $0.7 \times \square = 0.56$ e $\square \times 0.01 = 0.03$ f $\square \times 0.5 = 0.1$

g $\square \times 0.01 = 0.006$ h $12 \times \square = 2.4$ i $\square \times 8 = 3.2$

explanation 4

11 Round each number to the nearest 100.

a   240   b   670   c   1155

d   960   e   350   f   950

g   1950   h   45   i   4051

12 Round each number to the nearest 10.

a   28   b   84   c   121

d   125   e   99   f   948

g   1004   h   1995   i   4

13 Round each number to the degree of accuracy given.

a   823 (nearest 100)   b   102 (nearest 10)   c   1678 (nearest 1000)

d   2590 (nearest 1000)   e   500 (nearest 1000)   f   20 999 (nearest 1000)

14 The number of people attending a football match is exactly 67 189.
Round the number to these degrees of accuracy.

a   the nearest 10   b   the nearest 100

c   the nearest 1000   d   the nearest 10 000

15 The number of people voting in a local election was exactly 1 628 599.

Round the number to these degrees of accuracy.

a the nearest million   b the nearest 100 000

c the nearest 10 000   d the nearest 1000

e the nearest 100   f the nearest 10

(explanation 5a) (explanation 5b)

16 Round each number to 1 decimal place.

a 23.69   b 1.82   c 9.94   d 6.97

e 19.93   f 19.98   g 19.95   h 100.04

17 Round each number to 2 decimal places.

a 41.671   b 80.0453   c 1.007   d 30.0045

e 3.333 333 3   f 6.666 666 66   g 9.999 999 9   h 100.0045

18 Use a calculator to do each calculation.
Write your answer to the number of decimal places (d.p.) given.

a 6 ÷ 9 (1 d.p.)   b 17 ÷ 11 (1 d.p.)   c 17 ÷ 11 (2 d.p.)

d 14 ÷ 17 (1 d.p.)   e 20 ÷ 100 (2 d.p.)   f 7 ÷ 9 (2 d.p.)

19 Use a calculator to find the area of each shape.
Give your answer to the nearest whole number.

a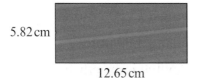

5.82 cm

12.65 cm

b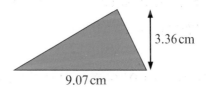

3.36 cm

9.07 cm

c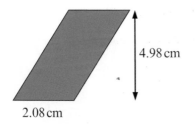

4.98 cm

2.08 cm

d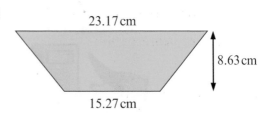

23.17 cm

8.63 cm

15.27 cm

Number N3.2

Mental methods (2)

- Knowing mental strategies for adding, subtracting, multiplying and dividing
- Converting between fractions, decimals and percentages
- Knowing mental strategies for solving problems involving fractions, decimals and percentages
- Estimating the square roots of non-square numbers
- Estimating the answer to calculations by rounding

Keywords

You should know

explanation 1a   explanation 1b

1 Work out these sums mentally.

    a   55 + 42   **b**   62 + 35   **c**   81 + 16   **d**   143 + 36

    e   351 + 28   **f**   475 + 38   **g**   726 + 77   **h**   326 + 685

2 Work out these subtractions mentally.

    a   76 − 54   **b**   84 − 21   **c**   97 − 63   **d**   156 − 22

    e   572 − 68   **f**   820 − 310   **g**   382 − 165   **h**   246 − 159

3 Work out, in your head, the change given for each item of shopping.

    a   A pen costing 48p and paid for using a £2.00 coin.

    b   A rubber costing 37p and paid for using a £1.00 coin.

    c   A magazine costing £1.70 and paid for using a £5.00 note.

    d   Some fruit costing £2.68 and paid for using a £5.00 note.

    e   A cap costing £4.65 and paid for using a £10.00 note.

    f   A CD costing £9.85 and paid for using a £20.00 note.

    g   Food costing £38.72 and paid for using a £50.00 note.

explanation 2

4 Work out these multiplications mentally.

    a 27×0.2 **b** 55×0.3 **c** 72×0.4 **d** 125×0.02

    e 320×0.04 **f** 410×0.05 **g** 228×0.02 **h** 820×0.04

5 a Serge's moneybox contains thirty-six 20p coins.
      How much money, in pounds, is this?

    b One biro costs 40p. Calculate the cost, in pounds, of buying sixty biros.

    c A sausage machine produces one hundred and twenty sausages each hour.
      Each sausage is 8 cm long. Calculate the total length, in metres, of sausages
      produced in 1 hour.

    d Beverley's footprint is 15 cm long. If she walks so that her footsteps lie end
      to end, calculate the total distance, in metres, walked after two hundred and
      eighty footsteps.

6 Without using a calculator work out these multiplications.

    a 13×1.4 **b** 16×1.3 **c** 22×2.1 **d** 44×3.2

    e 52×1.8 **f** 61×2.5 **g** 140×1.2 **h** 260×2.4

7 Work these out.

    a The total cost, in pounds, of 16 magazines at £1.20 each.

    b The total length of 30 cars, each 4.2 m long.

    c The total weight of 160 chocolate bars weighing 1.2 kg each.

    d The total cost in pounds of 81 sandwiches costing £2.10 each.

explanation 3

8 Work these out.

    a 23×11 **b** 16×11 **c** 32×12 **d** 45×19

    e 65×19 **f** 125×12 **g** 140×18 **h** 123×19

9 Work these out.

    a   The total number of pupils in 22 classes of 31 pupils each.

    b   The area of a rectangle 32 cm long and 19 cm wide.

    c   The area of a square garden with edges of length 29 m.

    d   The number of chairs in a hall, when there are 29 rows and 15 chairs in each row.

explanation 4a	explanation 4b

10 Work these out.

a	$930 \div 15$		**b**	$612 \div 12$		**c**	$504 \div 18$
d	$288 \div 9$		**e**	$680 \div 20$		**f**	$1155 \div 21$
g	$784 \div 28$		**h**	$2688 \div 24$		**i**	$2214 \div 18$
j	$2079 \div 21$		**k**	$1550 \div 25$		**l**	$2256 \div 16$

11 Work these out.

    a   810 people are split equally into 15 groups.
How many people are there in each group?

    b   £8.16 is shared equally amongst 12 children.
How much does each child receive?

    c   A postman has 360 letters to deliver equally to 45 houses.
How many letters does each house receive?

    d   216 kg of flour is shared equally amongst 24 families.
How much flour does each family receive?

12 Work these out.

a	$21 \div 0.03$	**b**	$32 \div 0.04$	**c**	$36 \div 0.06$	**d**	$420 \div 0.7$
e	$240 \div 0.12$	**f**	$320 \div 0.8$	**g**	$210 \div 0.14$	**h**	$560 \div 0.20$

explanation 5a   explanation 5b   explanation 5c

13 Copy and complete this table without using a calculator.

Decimal	Fraction	Percentage
0.5	$\frac{1}{2}$	
0.25		
0.333…		
	$\frac{1}{10}$	
		20%
0.666…		
	$\frac{3}{4}$	
	$\frac{1}{8}$	
	$\frac{3}{8}$	
		80%
1.5		150%
1.2		
	$\frac{145}{100}$	
	$\frac{5}{2}$	

14 Work these out.

a 50% of 40   b 25% of 80   c $\frac{1}{10}$ of 120   d $\frac{3}{10}$ of 120

e 0.1 of 70   f 0.4 of 70   g 60% of 70   h $\frac{2}{3}$ of 93

i $\frac{1}{8}$ of 248   j $\frac{5}{8}$ of 248   k 120% of 50   l 160% of 90

m 240% of 60   n 175% of 100   o 2% of 110   p 105% of 6

15 Work these out without using a calculator.

    a In a school of 320 pupils, 45% are girls. How many girls are there?

    b In a typical family, $\frac{3}{8}$ of income is spent on food. If a family's monthly income is £1200, calculate how much is spent on food.

    c In a survey of 450 earthworms, it was found that 36% were over 6 cm in length. How many earthworms in the survey were over 6 cm long?

    d Due to high demand, a shop decides to increase the price of one of its games consoles by 11%. If the price was originally £180, calculate the new selling price.

    e A book store decides to reduce the price of its books by $\frac{1}{3}$. If a book was originally selling for £24.90, calculate the new sale price.

---

explanation 6

---

16 Use estimation to match the value of each square root to a number in the box.

    a $\sqrt{5}$ **b** $\sqrt{24}$ **c** $\sqrt{84}$

    d $\sqrt{108}$ **e** $\sqrt{77}$ **f** $\sqrt{2}$

    g $\sqrt{150}$ **h** $\sqrt{410}$ **i** $\sqrt{34}$

9.2		8.8		4.9
	10.4		20.2	5.8
	12.2	2.2		1.4

17 Use your answers to question **16** to help you write the approximate length of the side of a square with each area.

    a Area = 34 cm^2 **b** Area = 108 cm^2 **c** Area = 5 m^2

---

explanation 7a   explanation 7b

---

18 Estimate the answer to each calculation, showing your method clearly.

    a 62×39 **b** 71×48 **c** 108×99 **d** 321×148

    e $242 \div 62$ **f** $389 \div 47$ **g** $\dfrac{12 \times 31}{2}$ **h** $\dfrac{189 \times 211}{8}$

    i $8 \times \sqrt{17}$ **j** $\sqrt{52} \times \sqrt{14}$ **k** $\dfrac{\sqrt{15} \times 89}{4}$ **l** $\dfrac{\sqrt{125} \times \sqrt{67}}{\sqrt{15}}$

    m $23^2 \times \sqrt{6}$ **n** $\dfrac{31^2}{9 \times \sqrt{105}}$ **o** $19^2 \times 41^2 \times \sqrt{10}$ **p** $\left(\dfrac{1}{3}\right)^2 \times 385$

Written methods

- Written methods for adding, subtracting, multipying and dividing involving decimals.

Keywords

You should know

Unless stated otherwise, no calculators should be used in this topic.

explanation 1

1 Work out these additions.

a   25.1 + 13.6   b   126.2 + 31.7   c   826.4 + 3.9

d   431.8 + 9.2   e   34.9 + 3.06   f   459.7 + 28.36

g   69 + 837.26   h   0.38 + 640.99   i   47.06 + 60.98

2 Work these out.

a   42.2 + 3.4 + 18.2   b   12.9 + 8.3 + 18

c   102.37 + 19.62 + 0.04   d   1312 + 106.04 + 13.1

e   1406.7 + 19.38 + 1.06   f   26.9 + 0.1 + 127.32 + 3.88

explanation 2a   explanation 2b

3 Work out these subtractions.

a   48.3 − 26.1   b   98.7 − 13.7   c   68.2 − 46.3

d   142.8 − 17.4   e   826.5 − 7.9   f   312.4 − 286.7

g   319.07 − 4.4   h   382.06 − 291.77   i   62.4 − 27.25

4 Work these out.

a   412.98 − 12.3 − 2.04   b   308.64 − 14.11 − 19.01

c   901.3 − 312.4 − 27.01   d   38.7 + 123.9 − 3.04

e   67.4 + 33.12 − 91.3 + 48.04   f   104.9 − 3.06 + 72.7 − 81.92

5 a The heights of three pupils are 1.80 m, 1.76 m and 1.69 m.
Calculate the combined height of the three pupils.

b Four apples are weighed. Their masses are 0.15 kg, 0.21 kg, 0.09 kg and 0.2 kg.
Calculate their total mass.

c A car is parked in a garage
with dimensions as shown.

How much space is there
between the roof of the car
and the ceiling?

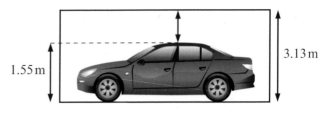

1.55 m

3.13 m

d A cave is 4.62 m tall. A stalactite
growing down from the ceiling is
1.38 m long, whilst a stalagmite
directly below it, is 0.87 m tall.

Calculate the distance between them.

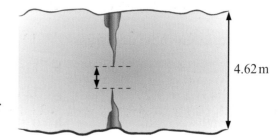

4.62 m

e Three crates, A, B and C, are arranged
in the back of a lorry which is
3.68 m long.

Crate A is 0.2 m long, crate B is 0.86 m
long and crate C is 1.05 m long.

Calculate the remaining length, *l*.

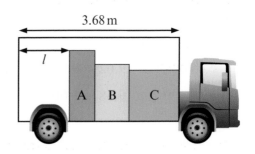

3.68 m

l

A B C

f Three packets X, Y and Z are weighed at the post
office. Their combined mass is 12.63 kg.

Y has a mass of 2.2 kg and Z has a mass of 6.49 kg.

Calculate the mass of packet X.

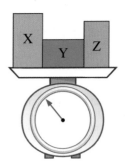

X Y Z

explanation 3a   explanation 3b

6 **i** Estimate the answer to each calculation.

ii Without using a calculator, work out each answer exactly.

a 32×2.5 **b** 820×4.1 **c** 98×4.7

d 125×3.62 **e** 178×12.4 **f** 168×14.6

*g 24.4×6.8 *h 34.4×28.3 *i 126.1×0.04

7 **a** 56.4 g of cake mix is used to make a cupcake. How much cake mix is needed for 62 cupcakes?

b The cost of a pencil is £0.18. Calculate the cost of buying 86 pencils.

c A magazine costs £2.42 per month. Calculate the cost of a year's subscription.

*d A rectangular garden is 23.4 m wide and 8.7 m long. Calculate its area.

explanation 4a   explanation 4b

8 Work these out.

a $92.8 \div 16$ **b** $178.2 \div 22$ **c** $223.2 \div 24$

d $225.6 \div 48$ **e** $387.2 \div 32$ **f** $566.1 \div 37$

9 Work out the answers to the following divisions.

a $32 \div 0.8$ **b** $3.64 \div 0.7$ **c** $153 \div 0.6$

d $0.345 \div 0.05$ **e** $31.14 \div 0.9$ **f** $0.739 \div 0.02$

g $531 \div 0.03$ **h** $0.741 \div 0.05$ **i** $4.36 \div 0.08$

10 The area of each shape is given. Calculate the unknown lengths.

a 16 cm Area = 60.8 cm² x

b 12.5 m Area = 80 m² x

Using a calculator

- Using a calculator for more complex calculations
- Writing answers in a format consistent with the question
- Converting time given in decimal format into hours, minutes and seconds

Keywords

You should know

explanation 1a   explanation 1b

1 Work out each answer using a calculator.
Check your answer by doing the calculation in your head.

a $\dfrac{6+4}{2}$

b $\dfrac{6}{2}+4$

c $6+\dfrac{4}{2}$

d $\dfrac{20-8}{4}$

e $\dfrac{20}{4}-8$

f $20-\dfrac{8}{4}$

g $\dfrac{5^2+15}{10}$

h $\dfrac{5^2}{10}+15$

i $5^2+\dfrac{15}{10}$

j $\dfrac{(12-8)^2}{2}$

k $\dfrac{12^2-8^2}{2}$

l $\dfrac{12^2}{2}-\dfrac{8^2}{2}$

2 Use a calculator to work these out.

a $\dfrac{3.6+2.1^2}{6-5.1}$

b $\dfrac{22^2-3.8^2}{17+8}$

c $\dfrac{48-(3.7+9.8)^2}{5}$

d $4.1\times(8.6-2.5)^2$

e $(3.2\times6.8)^2-(8.1\times2.1)^2$

f $\left(\dfrac{3.8}{19}\right)^2-3.6$

g $\dfrac{8.5}{10\times3.4}+6.2$

h $\sqrt{\dfrac{4.5\times8}{4}}$

i $\sqrt{\dfrac{28\times3}{4.2\times5}}+9$

3 The formula for converting degrees Celsius (°C) to degrees
Fahrenheit (°F) is $F=\dfrac{9}{5}C+32$.

a Use a calculator to convert these temperatures from °C to °F.

i 30°C   ii 18°C   iii 0°C

iv −5°C   v −40°C

b In order to estimate each answer, the formula can be
rewritten as $F\approx 2C+30$.

Without a calculator, estimate the answers to part **a**
using this formula.

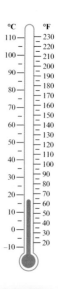

4 The formula for converting degrees Fahrenheit (°F) to degrees Celsius (°C) is
$C = \frac{5}{9}(F - 32)$.

a   Use a calculator to convert these temperatures from °F to °C.
Give your answers to 1 d.p.

   i 100°F   ii 70°F   iii 0°F   iv 32°F   v −40°F

b   In order to estimate each answer, the formula can be rewritten as
$C \approx \frac{1}{2}F - 15$.

Without a calculator, estimate the answers to part **a** using this formula.

---

explanation 2

Use the following information to answer questions **5–8**.
These were the approximate exchange rates
between pounds (£) and some other currencies
in December 2007.

£1 = 1.41 euros
£1 = 228.49 Japanese yen
£1 = 2.06 US dollars
£1 = 15.21 Chinese yuan

5 Assuming there are no additional bank charges, calculate how many pounds
would be exchanged for these amounts.

   a   1000 euros   b   500 US dollars

   c   10 000 Japanese yen   d   600 Chinese yuan

   e   400 euros and 8000 Japanese yen

   f   450 US dollars, 320 Chinese yuan and 6500 Japanese yen

6 a   How many US dollars would be exchanged for 500 euros?

   b   How many Chinese yuan would be exchanged for 650 Japanese yen?

   c   How many euros would be exchanged for 100 Japanese yen?

   d   How many US dollars would be exchanged for 10.20 Chinese yuan?

7 a A family of four pay $67 for a meal whilst on holiday in the USA. Calculate the cost of the meal in pounds.

b A couple pay 650 yuan for an extra tour whilst visiting China. Calculate the price of the tour in pounds.

c An American on holiday in Europe pays 86 euros for a train journey. Calculate the cost of the train in US dollars.

8 a Work out the new exchange rate for each of the currencies if the value of pounds increased by 15% .

b Work out the new exchange rate for each of the currencies if the value of pounds decreased by 7%.

(explanation 3)

9 Change each of these parts of a day into hours.

   a 0.5 of a day   **b** 0.75 of a day   **c** 0.625 of a day

10 Change each of these parts of an hour into minutes.

   a 0.2 of an hour   **b** 0.75 of an hour   **c** 0.85 of an hour

   d 0.66... of an hour   **e** 0.35 of an hour   **f** 0.95 of an hour

11 Change each of these times into hours and minutes.

   a 3.5 hours   **b** 4.75 hours   **c** 1.8 hours

   d 1.1 hours   **e** 7.65 hours   **f** 12.35 hours

12 A pupil spends $\frac{1}{3}$ of the day sleeping and $\frac{1}{10}$ of the day eating.

   a Calculate the total amount of time he spends either eating or sleeping. Give your answer in hours and minutes.

   b He spends $\frac{1}{4}$ of the remaining time playing with friends. How many hours and minutes is this?

13 Over a period of 5 hours in an evening, Katya spends $\frac{1}{4}$ of the time doing her homework, $\frac{1}{3}$ of her time watching television, $\frac{1}{8}$ of her time talking to friends on the phone and the rest of the time doing other things.

Calculate the following.

   a The amount of time in hours and minutes spent doing homework.

   b The amount of time in hours and minutes spent watching television.

   c The amount of time in hours and minutes spent talking to friends.

   d The fraction of her evening spent doing other things.

   e The time in hours and minutes spent doing other things.

14 The earth takes approximately 365 days (1 year) to orbit the sun. It therefore takes 365 days to do a full 360° rotation around the sun.

Calculate the number of days, hours and minutes the Earth takes to rotate the following number of degrees around the sun.

   a 180°   **b** 90°   **c** 10°

   d 1°   **e** 17°

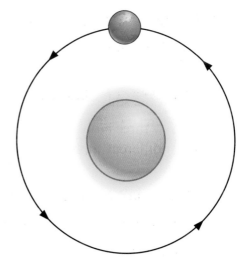

15 The Earth takes 24 hours (1 day) to rotate 360° on its axis.
Calculate the number of hours and minutes the Earth takes to rotate the following number of degrees on its axis.

   a 60°   **b** 45°   **c** 20°   **d** 1°   **e** 19°

Congruence

- Identifying congruent shapes, including and triangles and quadrilaterals

explanation 1

1 Draw a square like this on squared paper.

   a Split the square into two congruent shapes.

   b Draw three more of these squares.
Split each one into two congruent
shapes in a different way.

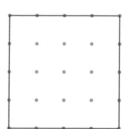

2 On squared paper, draw a square like the one in question **1**.

   a Split the square into four congruent shapes.

   b Draw three more of these squares. Split each one into four congruent shapes
in a different way.

3 Draw an equilateral triangle on isometric paper.

   a Split the triangle into three congruent shapes.

   b Draw three more of these triangles. Split each one into three congruent
shapes in a different way.

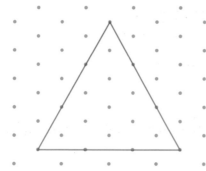

4 Which of these shapes are congruent to shape X?

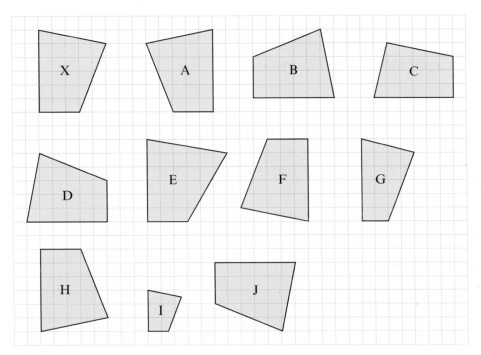

5 These two triangles are congruent.

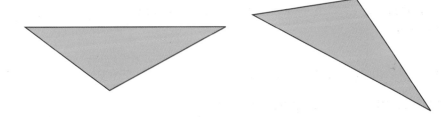

   a On card, draw two congruent scalene triangles without right angles.
      Cut them out.

   b Join your triangles so that two equal sides fit together.
      Make as many different shaes as you can. Draw each one.

   c Name each of the shapes that you drew in part **b**.
      Explain how you know.

6 Repeat question **5** for two congruent scalene triangles that have right angles.

Reflection, rotation and translation

- Carrying out combinations of reflections, rotations and translations
- Finding the symmetry properties of two-dimensional shapes

Keywords

You should know

explanation 1a   explanation 1b   explanation 1c

1 Copy each diagram. Reflect each shape in the line $x = 2$.

a

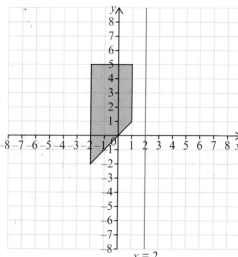

b

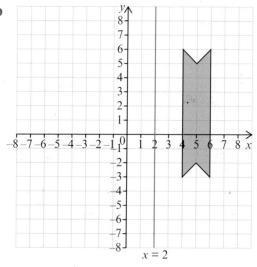

2 Copy each diagram. Reflect each shape in the line $y = x$.

a

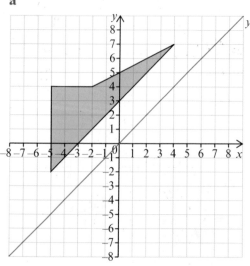

b

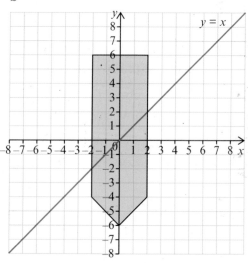

explanation 2a   explanation 2b

3 Copy each diagram. Rotate each shape 180° about (0, 0).

a

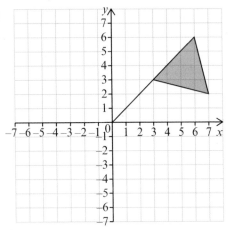

b

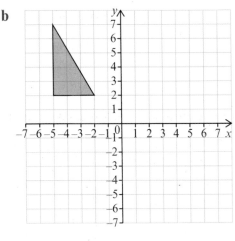

4 Copy each diagram. Rotate each shape 90° anticlockwise about the point shown.

a

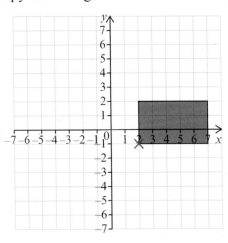

b

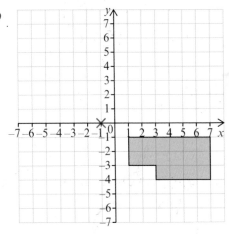

5 In each diagram, shape B is the image of object A after a single rotation.
Describe each rotation fully.

a

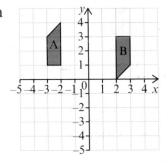

b

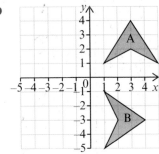

explanation 3a   explanation 3b

6 Copy each diagram. Translate each shape by the translation given.

a   Translation $\begin{pmatrix} 5 \\ -8 \end{pmatrix}$

b   Translation $\begin{pmatrix} -4 \\ -7 \end{pmatrix}$

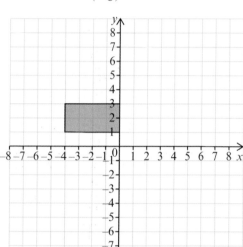

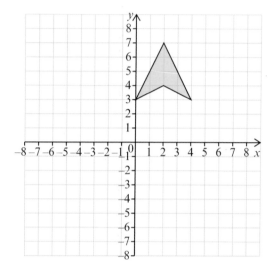

7 a   X has been translated to each of the shapes A, B, C and D.
Describe the translation that has taken place each time.
The first one has been done for you.

X to A: translation $\begin{pmatrix} 4 \\ 2 \end{pmatrix}$

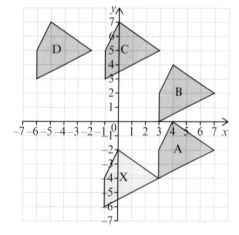

b   Describe the translation A to B. Explain how you could work out this
translation from your answers to part **a**, without using a diagram.

explanation 4a   explanation 4b

8 Copy each diagram. Reflect each shape in the *x*-axis and then reflect each image in the *y*-axis.

a

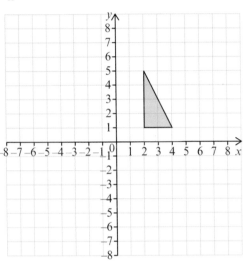

b

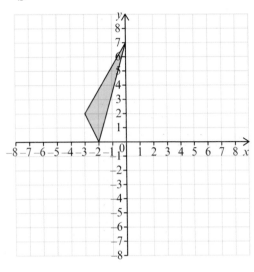

c

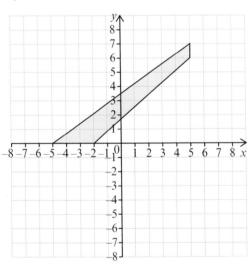

d

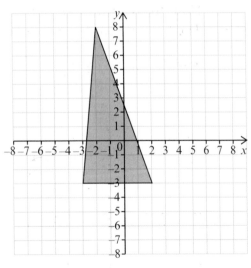

9 Look at your answers to question **8**.

What is the equivalent transformation for each combination of reflections?

10 Copy the diagrams in question **8**.

Reflect each shape in the *y*-axis and then reflect each image in the *x*-axis.

11 Look at your answers to question **10**.
What is the equivalent transformation for each combination of reflections?

12 Copy the diagram.

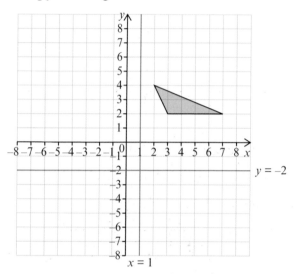

a Reflect the shape in the line $x = 1$ then reflect the image in the line $y = -2$.

b What is the equivalent single transformation?

13 Copy the diagram.

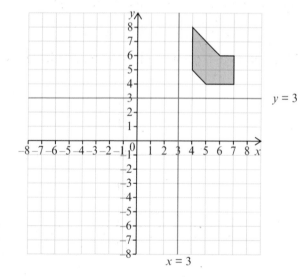

a Reflect the shape in the line $y = 3$ then reflect the image in the line $x = 3$.

b What is the equivalent single transformation?

14 Copy this diagram onto squared paper.

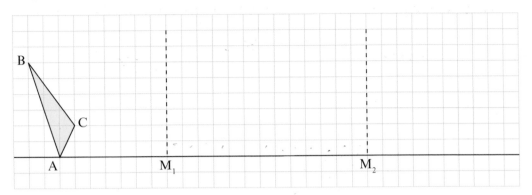

a   Reflect shape ABC in the mirror line M_1. Label the image A'B'C'.

b   Reflect image A'B'C' in the mirror line M_2. Label the object A"B"C".

c   What do you notice about the lengths AA" and M_1M_2?

d   What single transformation is equivalent to the two reflections?

15 On squared paper, draw a right-angled, scalene triangle.

    a   **i** Rotate your triangle 180° about the midpoint of its longest side.

       ii What shape have you made from the triangle and its image?

      iii Which angles are equal? Which sides are equal? Why do you think this is?

    b   **i** Rotate your triangle 180° about the midpoint of its shortest side.

       ii What shape have you made from the triangle and its image?

      iii Which angles are equal? Which sides are equal? Why do you think this is?

16 Write the coordinates of vertex A after translation 6 units right and then reflection in the x-axis.

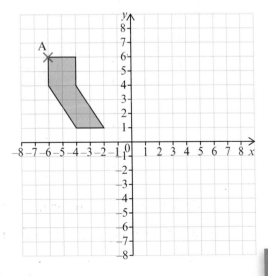

17 Copy these diagrams. Draw the image of each shape after it has undergone the set of transformations given. Mark the image of point A and label it A'.

a   Reflection in the *y*-axis and then translation $\begin{pmatrix} -4 \\ -2 \end{pmatrix}$.

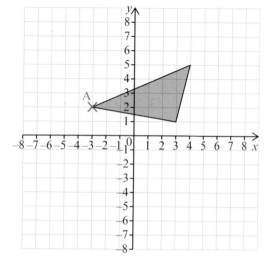

b   Rotation 90° clockwise, centre (0, 0), and then translation $\begin{pmatrix} 5 \\ 3 \end{pmatrix}$.

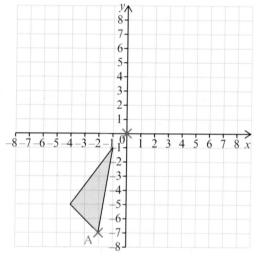

c   Rotation 180° with centre (1, 0), then reflection in the *x*-axis, and then translation $\begin{pmatrix} -4 \\ -4 \end{pmatrix}$.

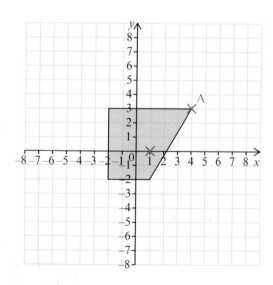

18 Repeat question **17**, but this time carry out the transformations in the reverse order. What do you notice about your answers compared to your answer to question **17**?

19 Find a combination of two transformations that will map these triangles onto each other.

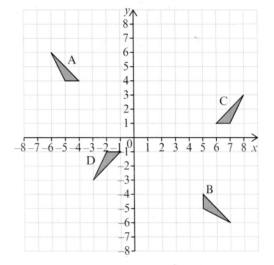

a   A onto C

b   A onto D

c   B onto C

d   C onto D

20 Write the single equivalent transformation for each of these repeated transformations. Give examples to show your answers are correct.

a   Two rotations about the same centre

b   Two translations

c   Reflection in two parallel lines

d   Reflection in two perpendicular lines

explanation 5a   explanation 5b

21 These shapes have different symmetry properties.

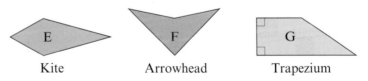

A   Rectangle   B   Parallelogram   C   Rhombus   D   Isosceles trapezium

E   Kite   F   Arrowhead   G   Trapezium

Copy and complete this symmetry table for the shapes.

		Number of lines of symmetry		
		0	1	2
Rotation symmetry	None		D	
	Order 2			

22 Copy these shapes.

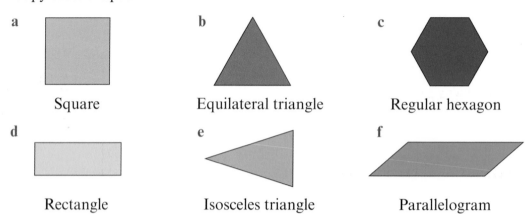

a Square

b Equilateral triangle

c Regular hexagon

d Rectangle

e Isosceles triangle

f Parallelogram

   i Mark any lines of symmetry on each shape.

  ii State the order of rotation symmetry of each shape.

23 State the order of rotation symmetry of these shapes.

   a regular pentagon   **b** regular octagon   **c** circle

24 The diagrams show incomplete mosaic patterns.
Each pattern has 4 coloured tiles missing.
Copy and complete the patterns so that they have
the stated symmetry properties.

   a Two lines of reflection symmetry, and rotation symmetry of order 2.

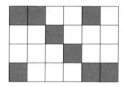

   b One line of reflection symmetry, and rotation symmetry of order 1.

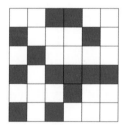

Enlargement

- Enlarging an object
- Describing enlargements

Keywords

You should know

explanation 1a   explanation 1b

1 Calculate each scale factor of enlargement.

a

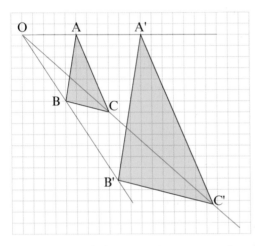

b

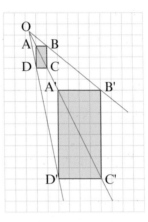

2 In each diagram, an object and a centre of enlargement O are shown. Copy each diagram and enlarge the object by the given scale factor.

a   Enlargement scale factor 3

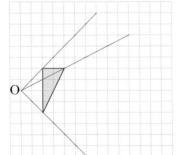

b   Enlargement scale factor 5

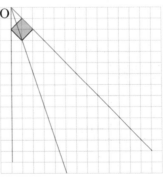

3 Copy these diagrams and enlarge each object by the scale factor shown. The centre of enlargement is marked O.

   a Enlargement scale factor 2

                                b Enlargement scale factor 2

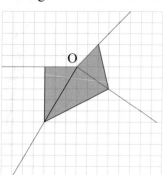
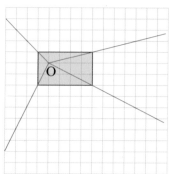

4 An object and its image are shown on each of the axes.

    i What are the coordinates of the centre of each enlargement?

    ii What is the scale factor of each enlargement?

a

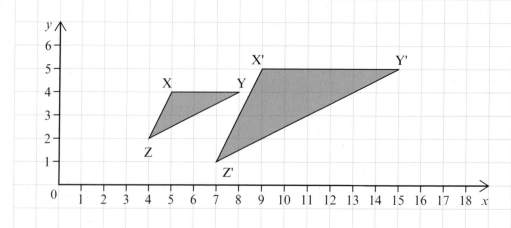

b

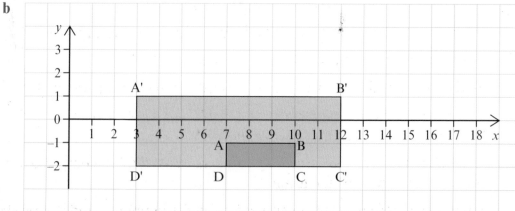

5 The diagram below shows an object 1 and several enlargements. Image 2 is an enlargement of 1 by scale factor 2. Image 3 is an enlargement of 1 by scale factor 3 etc. The centre of enlargement O is at the origin.

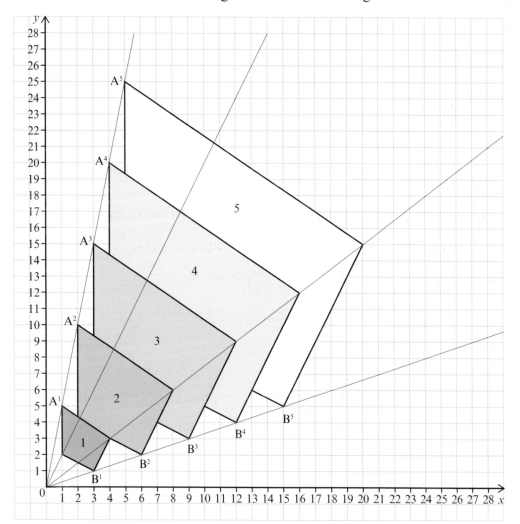

a What are the coordinates of A^1, A^2, A^3, A^4 and A^5?

b Predict the coordinates of A^6 and A^{10}. What are the coordinates of A^n?

c What are the coordinates of B^1, B^2, B^3, B^4 and B^5?

d Predict the coordinates of B^6 and B^{10}. What are the coordinates of B^n?

e An image of object 1 has coordinates (15, 75) for the A vertex.
What is the scale factor of the enlargement?

f What do you notice about the length of a side in the object compared to the corresponding sides of the images?

g What do you notice about corresponding angles in object 1 and the images?

125

Surveys

- Knowing different forms that data can take
- Testing a theory
- Identifying inappropriate questions in a survey
- Sampling a population
- Using two-way tables to record data

Keywords

You should know

explanation 1

1 Decide which of the following types of data are qualitative and which are quantitative.

   a   The number of pupils in a class

   b   The hair colour of pupils in your class

   c   The amount of time spent doing homework

   d   The weight of pupils' school bags

   e   The temperature of your classroom

   f   Your friends' opinions on the TV they watched last night

   g   The taste of the food that you ate for dinner last night

   h   The price of a bus ticket

2 For each activity describe one variable that is

      i a quantitative measure   ii a qualitative measure

   a   Paul does a crossword each day.

   b   Maria chooses a pair of trainers.

   c   Ahmed plays a computer game.

   d   Zak cycles to school each day.

   e   Amy's dad went shopping on Saturday.

   f   Pedro's grandmother sent him a parcel for his birthday.

   g   Carla's class went on a school trip yesterday.

   h   Simon ate a cake for lunch.

3 For each of the following, decide whether the variable is a discrete or a
continuous measure.

a   The temperature of a classroom

b   The shoe size of pupils in your class

c   The amount of pocket money received by pupils each week

d   The height of teachers in your school

e   The weight of school bags carried by pupils in your class

f   The number of pages in a maths textbook

g   The time it takes pupils to get to school in the morning

h   The speed of runners in a 100 m race

i   The speed at which secretaries can type

explanation 2

4 Data needs to be collected to test these theories.

Write the following for each theory.

  i   A description of data that could be collected to test the theory.

  ii A source for the data and whether it is a primary or secondary source.

a   Boys are taller than girls at secondary school.

b   Most people in the UK have internet access at home.

c   People recycle half of their household waste.

d   Sporty pupils have faster reaction times than non-sporty pupils.

e   Girls spend longer on homework than boys at secondary school.

f   Parents of pupils in your school believe that more homework should be set.

g   Children don't like to eat vegetables.

h   People prefer to go abroad for their summer holidays.

i   A cup of tea cools down more quickly if it is in a smaller cup.

explanation 3a   explanation 3b

5 Children's eating habits are being surveyed.

  i Identify what is wrong with each question.

  ii Suggest a better way to ask each question.

a Are you fat?   Yes ☐   No ☐   Not sure ☐

b What is your favourite food?   Pizza ☐   Burger ☐   Other ☐

c How old are you?   1–5 ☐   5–10 ☐   10–15 ☐   15–20 ☐

d Do you like fruit and vegetables?   Yes ☐   No ☐

e What is your favourite TV programme?

f Fried food is bad for you. Do you like fried food?   Yes ☐   No ☐   Some ☐

g On average how many calories do you eat a day?

6 The school canteen wants to conduct a survey to decide what to sell at break and lunchtime. It is not possible to ask every pupil. Suggest a way pupils could be sampled.

Remember to try to avoid bias in your sample.

7 A political party wants to know the voting intentions of adults in your area. Suggest a way in which the local population could be sampled.

8 For each of these surveys

  i identify the population

  ii suggest how you could select a sample

a Find out how pupils in your school travel to school.

b Find out how much people paid for their train tickets on a particular train.

c Find out how much people pay for their train tickets one day.

d Compare the ages of people shopping at different times of the day.

e Find out about local views on a housing development to be built in the area.

f Compare the ages of people buying different types of car.

g Find out the musical tastes of your friends.

h Find out about the length of time dogs are kept in a local dog's home.

explanation 4a   explanation 4b

9 You are to carry out a test to see if a certain 6-sided dice is biased. You will roll the dice 50 times and record the results in a table.

  a Draw a suitable table for recording the results.

  b Carry out the experiment and record the results in your table.

  c Based on your results, explain whether you think the dice you used is biased.

10 A survey is to be carried out to compare the heights of boys and girls in your class. These are three possible tables in which to record the results.

Height (cm)	Number of girls	Number of boys
135		
136		
137		
138		
139		
140		
141		
142		
143		
144		
145		
146		
147		
etc		

Height (cm)	Number of girls	Number of boys
120–130		
130–140		
140–150		
150–160		
160–170		
170–180		

Height (cm)	Number of girls	Number of boys
$120 < h \le 130$		
$130 < h \le 140$		
$140 < h \le 150$		
$150 < h \le 160$		
$160 < h \le 170$		
$170 < h \le 180$		

  a Explain, giving reasons, why the first table is not appropriate.

  b Explain, giving reasons, why the second table is not appropriate.

  c Explain, giving reasons, why the third table is the most appropriate.

  d Collect the heights of the pupils in your class and record them in the table.

  e Comment on the results of your data collection.

11 A survey is to be carried out to find out approximately how long pupils take to travel to school and also how they travel to school each morning. Below are three possible tables in which to record the results.

Time (min)	Walk	Bus	Car	Taxi	Bicycle	Other
$0 < T \leq 5$						
$5 < T \leq 15$						
$15 < T \leq 17$						
$17 < T \leq 25$						
$25 < T \leq 50$						

Time (min)	Walk	Bus	Car	Taxi	Bicycle	Other
$0 < T \leq 10$						
$10 < T \leq 20$						
$20 < T \leq 30$						
$30 < T \leq 40$						
$40 < T \leq 50$						

Time (min)	Walk	Bus	Car	Taxi	Bicycle	Other
0–10						
10–20						
20–30						
30–40						
40–50						

a Which of these tables is the most appropriate to use? Give reasons for your answer.

b Carry out the survey amongst pupils in your class and record the results in the table.

c What conclusions can you make from the data you have collected?

Analysing data (1)

- Understanding that statistics can be misleading
- Calculating the mean, median and mode from a frequency diagram
- Constructing a stem and leaf diagram
- Calculating the range, mean, median and mode from a stem and leaf diagram

Keywords

You should know

explanation 1a explanation 1b

1 Ten pupils scored these marks out of 15 in a mental arithmetic test.

8, 15, 13, 13, 9, 10, 12, 8, 9, 13

Calculate these statistics for the scores.

a the range   b the mode   c the mean   d the median

2 These are the masses in kilograms of 15 rugby players.

81, 110, 92, 95, 115, 118, 99, 95, 100, 102, 88, 89, 100, 111, 103

Work out these statistics for the masses.

a the range   b the mode   c the mean   d the median

3 An Olympic 100 m sprinter ran these times, measured in seconds, in her last eight competitive races.

12.82, 12.79, 12.02, 12.01, 12.88, 12.05, 12.52, 11.99

Work out these statistics for the times.

a the range   b the mode   c the mean   d the median

4 The five players in a 5-a-side hockey team have these masses in kilograms.

60, 64, 58, 57, 61

a Calculate the total mass of the five players.

b Calculate the mean mass of the five players.

The mean mass of the five players and the substitute is 61 kg.

c Calculate the total mass of the six players.

d Calculate the mass of the substitute.

5 Peter and Amelia play three games. Some of their scores are given in the table.

Their scores have the same mean.

The range of Peter's scores is twice that of Amelia's scores.

Copy and complete the table.

Peter		44	
Amelia	38	45	49

---

explanation 2

---

6 Tony scored these marks out of 20 in his last eight maths tests.

4, 5, 20, 20, 3, 6, 2, 7

a For this set of scores, calculate these averages.

    i the mean   **ii** the median   **iii** the mode

b Tony says that his average test score is 20. Is this true?

c In this case, which average is the best indicator of his results? Give reasons for your answer.

7 A manufacturer of batteries tests the life of the batteries by testing ten batteries. They lasted for these numbers of hours.

14.5, 16.2, 17.1, 3.3, 16.0, 17.2, 17.8, 3.3, 18.1, 17.0

a Find these averages for the ten batteries tested. Give your answers in hours and minutes.

    i the mean

    ii the median

    iii the mode

b A rival battery manufacturer claims that these results show that on average the batteries only last 3.3 hours. Is this claim true? Give reasons for your answer.

c Explain which is the most reliable form of average for this set of data.

explanation 3

8 The shoe sizes of 30 pupils in a class are shown in the bar chart.

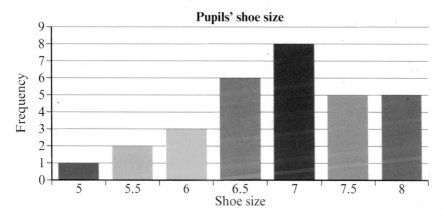

a How many pupils have a shoe size of 6?

b Calculate the mean shoe size of the 30 pupils.

c Find the median shoe size of the pupils.

d State the modal shoe size of the pupils.

9 Reviewers were asked to preview a film and give it a rating from 1 to 5.
The responses are shown in the bar-line chart (1 means awful, 5 means excellent).

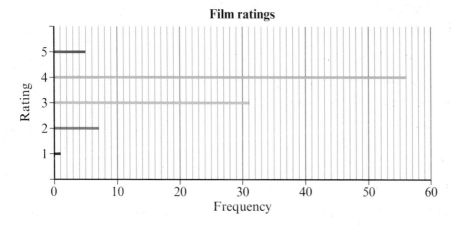

a How many people took part in the survey?

b How many people rated the film excellent?

c Calculate the mean rating for the film.

d Find the median rating for the film.

e Calculate the modal rating for the film.

explanation 4

10 25 caterpillars were measured. The lengths in millimetres are shown in this stem and leaf diagram.

```
0 | 9
1 | 2 2 4 7 9
2 | 1 1 3 4 5 5 7 8 8 9          Key: 2|1 represents a length of 21 mm
3 | 3 3 4 5 6 6 6
4 | 1 1
```

a   Write the length of the shortest and the longest caterpillars measured.

b   Find the modal caterpillar length.

c   What is the median caterpillar length?

11 20 girls and 20 boys sat the same maths test. These are their results out of 50.

Girls: 28, 32, 26, 21, 33, 33, 42, 7, 12, 14, 28, 50, 48, 14, 20, 38, 33, 32, 27, 22
Boys: 37, 26, 32, 32, 27, 2, 36, 7, 27, 33, 33, 36, 5, 7, 37, 36, 12, 31, 32, 12

a   Draw a stem and leaf diagram for the girls' results and another for the boys' results.

b   Write the modal results for the girls and for the boys.

c   Find the median result for the girls and for the boys.

d   Calculate the range of the girls' results and the range of the boys' results.

e   Calculate the mean result for the girls and the mean result for the boys.

f   Use your answers to help you write a short paragraph comparing the girls' and boys' results.

Representing data

- Drawing a pie chart by calculating the degrees for each sector
- Drawing bar charts or frequency diagrams as appropriate for discrete and continuous data
- Drawing and interpreting simple line graphs
- Drawing and interpreting scatter graphs

Keywords

You should know

explanation 1

1 A survey was carried out to find the favourite pets of pupils in one year. 36 pupils were asked.

The pie chart shows the results.

a How many degrees represent one pupil?

b How many degrees of the pie chart represent pupils who said dogs were their favourite pet?

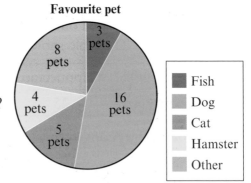

Favourite pet

3 pets
8 pets
4 pets
16 pets
5 pets

Fish
Dog
Cat
Hamster
Other

c What fraction of pupils said hamsters were their favourite pet? Give your answer in its simplest form.

d Construct the pie chart accurately, showing the degrees in each section.

2 The table shows the results of a survey to find out how people usually travel to their local shopping centre.

Mode of transport	Walk	Cycle	Bus	Car	Other
Frequency	3	12	70	80	15

180 people were asked. The results are to be shown in a pie chart.

a How many degrees will represent each person in the survey?

b How many degrees of the pie chart will represent those who usually travel by bus?

c What fraction of people surveyed said they usually cycle? Give your answer in its simplest form.

d Construct the pie chart accurately, showing the degrees in each section.

3 A class of 30 pupils was surveyed to find out what their favourite lesson was. The results are shown in the table.

Subject	English	Maths	Science	P.E.	Drama	Other
Frequency	2	10	6	7	3	2

   a How many degrees of a pie chart will represent each pupil?

   b How many degrees of a pie chart will represent the pupils who said maths was their favourite subject?

   c Draw and label a pie chart to display the results of the survey.

explanation 2a   explanation 2b

4 A coffee shop carried out a survey to see what type of coffee their customers like drinking. The table shows the results.

Type of coffee	Cappuccino	Latte	Filter	Espresso	Other
Frequency	25	17	8	4	6

   a How many people were surveyed in total?

   b Construct a bar chart to show this data.

   c Draw a pie chart to show the data.

   d Which chart do you think shows the data more clearly? Give a reason for your answer.

5 Thirty children were asked how much time they spend watching television on average each week. The results are given in this grouped frequency table.

Time (hours)	Frequency
$0 \leq T < 2$	6
$2 \leq T < 4$	1
$4 \leq T < 6$	4
$6 \leq T < 8$	9
$8 \leq T < 10$	5
$10 \leq T < 12$	5

   a Draw a grouped frequency diagram for the data.

   b What is the modal time group?

6 50 pupils are timed running 400 m. The results are shown in the table.

Time (s)	$60 \leq T < 70$	$70 \leq T < 80$	$80 \leq T < 90$	$90 \leq T < 100$	$100 \leq T < 110$
Frequency	2	6	28	13	1

   a Explain what is meant by the time $90 \leq T < 100$.

   b Draw a frequency diagram for these results.

7 Some of the world's mountains that are higher than 8000 m are listed below.

Mountain peak	Location	Height (m)
Everest	China/Nepal/Tibet	8850
K2	Pakistan/China	8611
Kanchenjunga	India/Nepal	8586
Lhotse I	China/Nepal/Tibet	8516
Makalu I	China/Nepal/Tibet	8463
Cho Oyu	China/Nepal/Tibet	8201
Dhaulagiri	Nepal	8167
Nanga Parbat	Pakistan	8163
Annapurna	Nepal	8091
Gasherbrum I	Pakistan/China	8068
Broad Peak	Pakistan/China	8047
Gasherbrum II	Pakistan/China	8035
Shisha Pangma	China	8013

   a Copy and complete the grouped frequency table.

   b Draw a frequency diagram showing the heights of the world's tallest mountains.

   c Which is the modal height group?

Height (m)	Frequency
$8000 \leq H < 8200$	
$8200 \leq H < 8400$	
$8400 \leq H < 8600$	
$8600 \leq H < 8800$	
$8800 \leq H < 9000$	

explanation 3

8 The graph below shows the temperature in degrees Celsius (°C) at a holiday resort over a 24-hour period.

Temperature readings were taken every 4 hours.

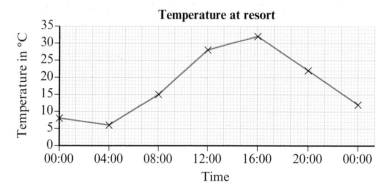

a What was the temperature at noon?

b What was the lowest temperature recorded over the 24-hour period?

c Is it possible that the temperature rose above 32 °C on that day? Explain your answer.

9 A class at a primary school decide to see how many millimetres of rain fell over a 10-week period. The reading for the total rainfall is recorded every seven days, as shown in the table.

Days	7	14	21	28	35	42	49	56	63	70
Total rainfall (mm)	2	2	8	10	10	10	23	25	26	28

a Draw a line graph to show the total amount of rainfall over the 10-week period.

b **i** In which weeks was there no rain?

  ii Explain how you got your answer to part **i**.

c **i** In which week was there the most rain?

  ii Explain how you got your answer to part **i**.

d Calculate the average weekly rainfall during the 10-week period.

e From your graph estimate the total amount of rain that had fallen by the 45th day.

10 The table gives the median weight of baby girls from 0 to 36 months.

Age (months)	0	3	9	15	24	36
Weight (kg)	3.4	5.6	8.4	10.3	12.0	13.8

   a Plot a line graph of the median weight of baby girls from 0 to 36 months.

   b Estimate from your graph the median weight of a 12-month baby girl.

   c A doctor is checking the weight of a baby girl who is 20 months old. The doctor weighs her and records her weight as 11.8 kg. Use your graph to determine whether the girl is heavier than the median weight for her age.

11 The table shows the total UK population from 1950 and projected forward to 2050 .

Year	Population (millions)
1950	50.1
1960	52.3
1970	55.6
1980	56.2
1990	57.5
2000	59.5
2010	61.3
2020	63.1
2030	64.3
2040	64.5
2050	64.0

   a Construct a line graph showing the total population of the UK from 1950 to 2050.

   b Use your line graph to estimate the total UK population in 2008.

   c One decade was described as the 'baby boom' years. From your graph work out in which decade the baby boom occurred.

   d Justify your answer to part **c**.

explanation 4a | explanation 4b

12 A group of 15 pupils sat a maths and a science test. Their percentage scores are shown in the table.

Maths %	98	55	27	38	82	77	64	12	62	68	84	55	36	90	60
Science %	88	60	34	38	75	81	70	20	65	55	92	60	30	100	72

   a Draw a scatter graph of the science results plotted against the maths results.

   b State whether you agree or disagree with the following statements.

      i All pupils with at least 60% in maths scored at least 60% in science.

      ii Most pupils with at least 60% in maths scored at least 60% in science.

      iii All pupils with less than 40% in maths scored less than 40% in science.

   c How many pupils scored less than 50% in maths?

13 A motorist puts 60 litres of petrol in her car. Every 100 km travelled she records the amount of petrol in her tank. The readings are given in the table.

Distance (km)	0	100	200	300	400	500	600	700	800
Petrol in tank (litres)	60	55	48	42	35	27	21	15	9

She then plots a scatter graph of the amount of petrol left against the distance travelled.

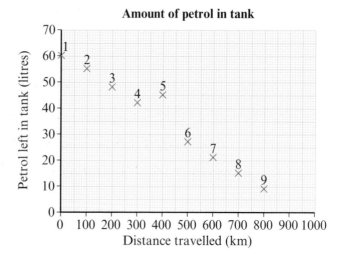

Amount of petrol in tank

   a One of the points is plotted incorrectly. Which is it?

   b Plot an accurate scatter graph of the results.

   c Is there a relationship between distance travelled and the amount of petrol left?

Interpreting data

- Interpreting different types of graph
- Giving reasons to justify your answers
- Deciding whether a graph displays its data clearly

Keywords

You should know

explanation 1

1 This graph shows crime statistics relating to vehicle theft since 1981.

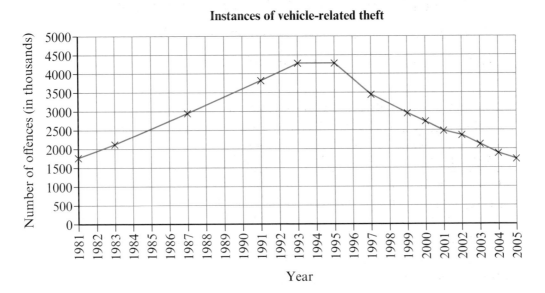

Instances of vehicle-related theft

a Approximately how many vehicle-related thefts were reported in 2005?

b Which years showed the highest theft figures?

c Write a short paragraph describing what the graph shows.

d Give a possible reason for the drop in vehicle-related thefts since 1995.

2 Each graph shows the overall crime figures between April 2005 and March 2006 for one particular region compared to the national averages.

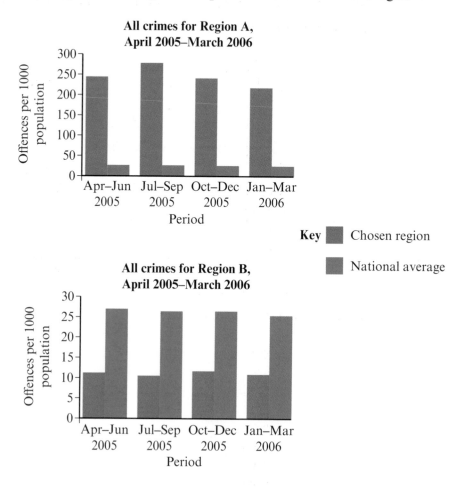

Key — Chosen region

— National average

a Approximately how many offences on average were committed per thousand of the population nationally between January and March 2006?

b Approximately how many offences were committed per thousand of the population in Region B between January and March 2006?

c Approximately how many offences were committed per thousand of the population in Region A between January and March 2006?

d Write a short paragraph describing any similarities and differences between the crime figures for the two regions.

e Explain whether you think the graphs are clear. Justify your answer.

3 These graphs show the 2007 population pyramids for two different countries.

The numbers in the middle of the pyramids represent the ages of the population.

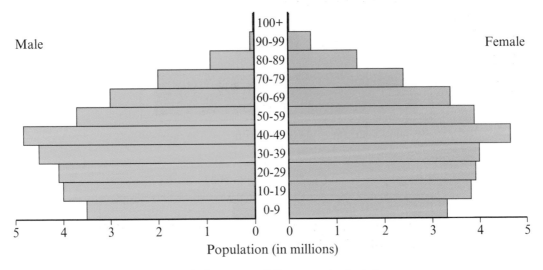

Population pyramid for a country in Europe

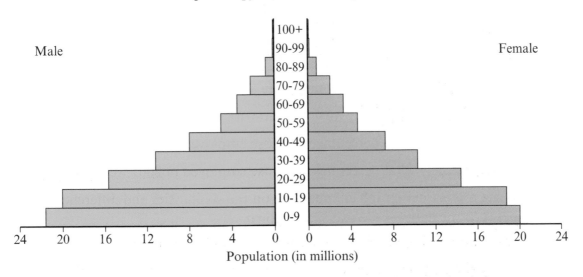

Population pyramid for a country in Asia

a Approximately how many 0−9 year old girls were there in the Asian country in 2007?

b Approximately how many 0−9 year old girls were there in the European country in 2007?

c In the Asian country which age group had the most people?

d In the European country which age group had the most people?

e Write a short paragraph describing some of the differences and similarities between the two graphs.

4 These two graphs show the numbers of unemployed males and females taken from Census data for a city in 1931 and 2001.

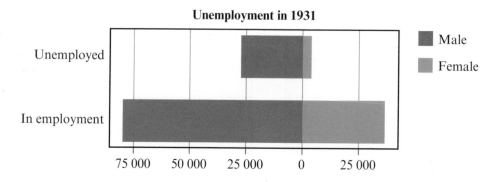

Unemployment in 1931

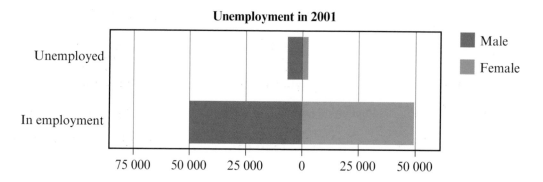

Unemployment in 2001

a Approximately how many women were at work in 1931?

b Approximately how many men were at work in 1931?

c Approximately what percentage of those employed in 1931 were women?

d Approximately what percentage of those employed in 2001 were women?

e Write a short paragraph commenting on the similarities and differences between the data for the two years shown.

Number N4.1

Order of operations

- Working out more complex calculations involving brackets and powers

Keywords

You should know

explanation 1

1 Calculate these without using a calculator.

a $4 + 5^2$

b $(4 + 5)^2$

c $4^2 + 5^2$

d $\dfrac{13 - 3^2}{5}$

e $\dfrac{(13 - 3)^2}{5}$

f $\left(\dfrac{13 - 3}{5}\right)^2$

g $16 - 2 \times 4$

h $(16 - 2) \times 4$

i $24 \div 3 + 5$

j $24 \div (3 + 5)$

k $(36 \div 6 + 12) \div 4$

l $36 \div (6 + 12 \div 4)$

m $36 \div 6 + 12 \div 4$

n $36 \div (6 + 12) \div 4$

o $(36 \div 6) + (12 \div 4)$

2 Calculate these without using a calculator.

a $12 - 3 \times 2$

b $(12 - 3) \times 2$

c $8^2 - 14 \div 2$

d $(8^2 - 14) \div 2$

e $(15 - 5)^2 \times 2 + 8$

f $15 - 5^2 \times (2 + 8)$

g $15 - 5^2 \times 2 + 8$

h $15 - (5^2 \times 2 + 8)$

i $(15 - 5^2) \times 2 + 8$

3 If necessary insert brackets in the following calculations in order to make them correct.

a $6 + 24 \div 6 + 4 = 14$

b $6 + 24 \div 6 + 4 = 9$

c $6 + 24 \div 6 + 4 = 3$

d $6 + 24 \div 6 + 4 = 8.4$

e $16 + 4^2 \times 8 - 3 = 3197$

f $16 + 4^2 \times 8 - 3 = 141$

g $16 + 4^2 \times 8 - 3 = 96$

h $16 + 4^2 \times 8 - 3 = 160$

4 The perimeter, P, of the rectangle shown is given by this formula.
$P = 2x + 2y$.

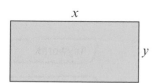

   a Write the formula for the perimeter of the rectangle using brackets.

   b Calculate the perimeter when $x = 6\,\text{cm}$ and $y = 3.5\,\text{cm}$.

5 The perimeter, P, of this triangle is given by
the formula $P = a + b + c$.

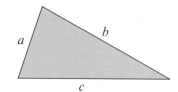

   a Write, using brackets, the formula for the
perimeter of a triangle whose sides are
double the length of these.

   b If $a = 3\,\text{cm}$, $b = 5\,\text{cm}$ and $c = 6\,\text{cm}$,
calculate the perimeter of the triangle
described in part **a**.

6 This square has edges of length $(m + n)\,\text{cm}$.

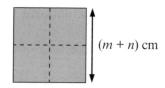

   a Using brackets, write a formula for the
perimeter, P, of the square.

   b Using brackets, write a formula for the
area, A, of the square.

   c The square is divided into four equal parts as shown.
Write an expression, using brackets, for the perimeter of each of the smaller
squares.

   d Write an expression for the area of each of the smaller squares.

   e When $m = 6$ and $n = 8$, calculate the values of each of the perimeters or
areas in parts **a–d** above.

Checking

- Spotting incorrect answers in a number of different situations

Keywords

You should know

explanation 1

1 In each pair of calculations, one is incorrect. Without using a calculator, identify which one must be the incorrect calculation. Give reasons for your choice.

a i $56 + 8 \div 8 = 8$ ii $56 + 8 \div 8 = 57$

b i $25 - 10 \times 2 = 30$ ii $25 - 10 \times 2 = 5$

c i $(14.1 - 3.8)^2 = 106.09$ ii $(14.1 - 3.8)^2 = 20.09$

d i $\dfrac{27.3 \times 2.9}{9.1} = 8.7$ ii $\dfrac{27.3 \times 2.9}{9.1} = 0.87$

e i $\dfrac{\sqrt{100 - 36}}{4} = 2$ ii $\dfrac{\sqrt{100 - 36}}{4} = 20$

f i $(20 - 15)^2 - 10 \div 5 = 3$ ii $(20 - 15)^2 - 10 \div 5 = 23$

g i $5 \times 4.9^2 = 600.25$ ii $5 \times 4.9^2 = 120.05$

h i $\dfrac{52 \div 5^2}{3.8} = 28.46$ ii $\dfrac{52 \div 5^2}{3.8} = 0.547$

2 Without using a calculator, pick out a possible answer to each calculation from the ones given. Give reasons for your choice.

a 58×60 i 3480   ii 348   iii 4080

b $4.98 \div 0.33$ i 1.66   ii 15.09   iii 0.92

c $327 \div 1.1$ i 297.27   ii 29.73   iii 327.11

d 1001×2.1 i 2001.1   ii 2102.1   iii 1999.1

3 a $\sqrt{x} = 22.5$.

Which of these methods is correct for finding x?

  i $x = 2 \times 22.5$ **ii** $x = 22.5^2$ **iii** $x = \sqrt{22.5}$

b $p^2 = 2116$.

Which of these methods is correct for finding p?

  i $p = 2116 \div 2$ **ii** $p = 2116^2$ **iii** $p = \sqrt{2116}$

c $(m - 25) \div 5 = 15$.

Which of these methods is correct for finding m?

  i $m = 15 \times 5 + 25$ **ii** $m = (15 + 25) \times 5$ **iii** $m = 15 + 5$

4 a Ali did a survey of eye colours with the 25 pupils in his class.
He produced this table of results showing the percentage in each category.

Eye Colour	Blue	Brown	Hazel	Green
Percentage	40%	30%	25%	15%

Explain why these results must be incorrect.

b Sarah repeated the survey with the same 25 pupils.
Her results are shown below.

Eye Colour	Blue	Brown	Hazel	Green
Percentage	40%	30%	14%	16%

Explain why her results must be incorrect as well.

5 The mass in kilograms of 10 pupils are given below.

45   38   52   55   51   48   50   49   41   53

The mean mass is calculated as 56 kg. Without calculating the mean, explain
why this value cannot possibly be correct.

$$\text{Mean} = \frac{\text{sum of all the values}}{\text{number of values}}$$

Ratios

- The relationship between fractions and ratios
- Simplifying ratios
- Dividing a quantity in a given ratio
- Using the unitary method to solve problems involving ratio

Keywords

You should know

explanation 1

1 Write the proportion of each shape that is coloured, as a fraction in its simplest form.

a

b
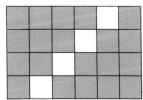

c
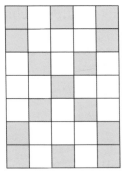

d
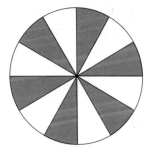

e

f
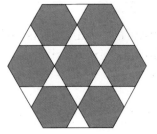

2 Write the ratio of coloured area to non-coloured area for each of the shapes in question 1.

3 The bar chart shows the number of GCSEs achieved by a group of 24 pupils.

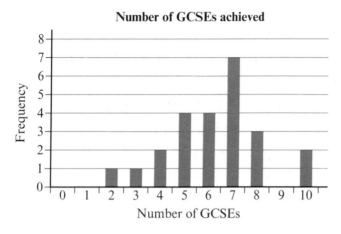

Number of GCSEs achieved

a   What proportion of the pupils achieved exactly 5 GCSEs?
    Give your answer as a fraction in its simplest form.

b   What proportion of the pupils achieved 5 or more GCSEs?
    Give your answer as a fraction in its simplest form.

c   What is the ratio of pupils achieving 5 GCSEs to pupils achieving other
    results?

d   What is the ratio of pupils achieving 5 or more GCSEs to pupils achieving
    fewer than 5 GCSEs?

4 The pie chart shows the eye colour of a group of 36 people.

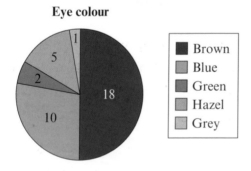

Eye colour

■	Brown
■	Blue
■	Green
■	Hazel
■	Grey

a   What proportion of the people have hazel eyes?

b   What is the ratio of people with hazel eyes to people with other coloured
    eyes?

c   What proportion of the people have either hazel or green eyes?

d   What is the ratio of people with green or hazel eyes to people with other
    coloured eyes?

explanation 2

5 Use the data on eye colour from question **4**.

   a What is the ratio of blue to hazel eye colours among the 36 people?
Give your ratio in its simplest form.

   b What is the ratio of blue to brown eye colours among these people?
Give your ratio in its simplest form.

   c One of the ratios of eye colour is given as $9:1$.
Which two eye colours are in this ratio?

6 Simplify these ratios.

   a $4:2$ **b** $8:6$ **c** $8:12$ **d** $5:15$

   e $16:24$ **f** $18:27$ **g** $6:72$ **h** $30:6$

   i $14:56$ **j** $28:21$ **k** $48:144$ **l** $49:63$

7 The following pairs of ratios are equivalent. Work out the unknown values.

   a $1:2 = 3:x$ **b** $7:21 = p:42$ **c** $2:5 = n:25$

   d $15:y = 45:18$ **e** $a:9 = 40:72$ **f** $6:18 = 5:b$

   g $1:2:3 = 5:m:n$ **h** $3:5:6 = p:30:q$ **i** $d:3:7 = 16:12:e$

explanation 3

8 The following ratios involve quantities with different units. Write both
quantities in the same units then simplify to give the ratio in its simplest form.

   a $2\,cm:5\,m$ **b** $8\,mm:12\,cm$ **c** $25\,g:3\,kg$

   d $6\,mm:5\,m$ **e** $4\,mm:1\,km$ **f** $15\,kg:2\,tonnes$

   g $125\,g:1\,tonne$ **h** $20\,s:5\,min$ **i** $5\,s:2\,hours$

   j $150\,mm:15\,km$ **k** $10\,min:3\,days$ **l** $40\,ml:10\,litres$

9 A model car is made to a scale of $1:50$.

   a The model has a length of $10\,cm$. Calculate the
length of the real car. Give your answer in metres.

   b The real car has a height of $1.75\,m$. Calculate the height of the model car.

10 In 2007, the Taipei Tower in Taiwan was the world tallest building, standing at a height of approximately 510 m.

    a On a photograph, the tower is 15 cm tall.
What is the scale of the photo to the real thing?
Write the ratio in its simplest form.

    b A poster is produced to a scale of 1 : 200.
Calculate the height of the tower on the poster.

11 A map is drawn to a scale of 1 : 50 000.

    a Calculate the real distance, if a distance on the map is 3 cm.
Give your answer in metres.

    b Calculate the distance on the map, if a distance on the ground is 8 km.
Give your answer in centimetres.

12 An architect produces a plan of a building to a scale of 1 : 25.

    a The height of the real building will be 8 m.
What height is the building on the plan? Give your answer in centimetres.

    b The length of the building on the plan is 45 cm.
Calculate the length of the actual building. Give your answer in metres.

explanation 4

13 A piece of string 24 cm long is divided into smaller pieces in these ratios.
Calculate the length of each of the smaller pieces.

    a 1 : 7   **b** 1 : 5   **c** 1 : 3   **d** 7 : 5

    e 5 : 19   **f** 5 : 3   **g** 1 : 2 : 3   **h** 3 : 5 : 4

14 A piece of wood 48 cm long is cut into smaller pieces in these ratios.
Calculate the length of each of the smaller pieces of wood.

    a 1 : 15   **b** 5 : 1   **c** 1 : 31   **d** 1 : 1 : 14

    e 1 : 2 : 3 : 6   **f** 3 : 5 : 4 : 4   **g** 6 : 8 : 5 : 3 : 2   **h** 8 : 12 : 7 : 5

15 Blue, white and yellow paint is mixed in the ratio 3:20:2.
The paint is sold in 5-litre containers.

Calculate the volume of each colour paint in the containers.

   a White paint   **b** Blue paint   **c** Yellow paint

16 A fruit juice is made from mango, orange, apple and grape juices in the ratio
4:8:3:1. The juice is sold in 1 litre cartons.

   a Calculate the amount of mango juice in a carton.

   b Calculate the amount of apple juice in a carton.

   c A promotional carton is produced with 25% extra free.
      Calculate the amount of orange juice used in a promotional carton.

17 P and Q are two chain wheels. For every 2 complete rotations that wheel P
makes, wheel Q makes 7.

   a If wheel P makes 250 rotations,
      calculate the number of rotations
      made by wheel Q.

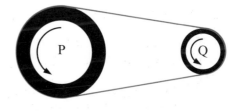

   b If wheel Q makes 497 rotations,
      calculate the number of rotations
      made by wheel P.

   c If the combined number of rotations is 1620, calculate the number of
      rotations made by each wheel.

18 A square has the same area as a rectangle.

   The sides of the rectangle are in the ratio 9:4.
   The perimeter of the rectangle is 130 cm.

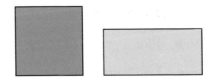

   a Calculate the lengths of the sides of
      the rectangle.

   b Calculate the area of the rectangle.

   c Calculate the side length of the square.

   d Write down the ratio of the perimeters of the two shapes in the form
      perimeter of square : perimeter of rectangle.
      Give your answer in its simplest form.

Graphs of real-life situations

- Properties of direct proportionality
- Using graphs to find the relationship between two variables
- Writing a ratio in the form 1 : n
- Converting a ratio to an equation linking two variables

Keywords

You should know

explanation 1a   explanation 1b

1 In December 2007, the exchange rate from pounds (£) to US dollars ($) was approximately 1 : 2. Therefore £1 could be exchanged for $2.

a Copy and complete this exchange rate table.

Pounds (£)	0	5	10	15	20
US dollars ($)		10			

b Plot a graph showing the relationship between pounds and dollars.

2 In August 2007, the exchange rate from pounds (£) to euros (€) was approximately 2 : 3. Therefore £2 could be exchanged for €3.

a Copy and complete this exchange rate table.

Pounds (£)	0	10	20	50	100
Euros (€)		15			

b Plot a graph to show the relationship between pounds and euros.

c Use your graph to estimate the number of pounds that would be exchanged for €45.

3 A car is driving at a constant speed. The table shows the total number of kilometres the car has travelled after different lengths of time.

Time (h)	0	1	2	3	4	5	6
Distance (km)			180		360	450	

a Calculate the speed, in km/h, of the car.

b Copy and complete the table.

$$\text{Speed} = \frac{\text{distance}}{\text{time}}$$

c Plot a graph showing the relationship between time and distance travelled.

d When the car is travelling at a constant speed, are time and distance directly proportional? How do you know?

e Use your graph to estimate the distance travelled after 3 hours 30 minutes.

explanation 2a   explanation 2b   explanation 2c

4 This graph can be used to convert between miles and kilometres.

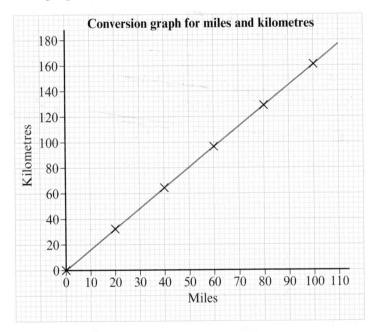

a From the graph find the number of kilometres equivalent to 100 miles.

b Find the number of kilometres in 1 mile.

c Use your answer to part **b** to calculate the number of kilometres in 70 miles.

d Find the number of miles equivalent to 1 kilometre.

e Use your answer to part **d** to calculate the number of miles in 250 km.

5 Write each ratio in the form $1:n$.

   a $2:5$ **b** $3:10$ **c** $4:5$ **d** $9:15$

   e $15:6$ **f** $25:6$ **g** $1.5:1$ **h** $9:5$

6 This graph can be used to convert between inches and centimetres.

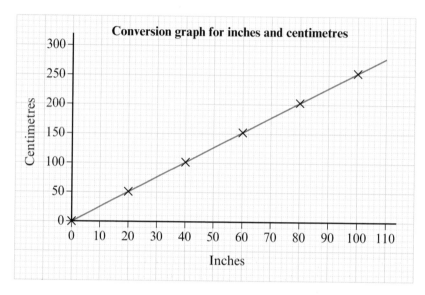

   a Use the graph to find the number of centimetres equivalent to 100 inches.

   b Calculate the number of centimetres equivalent to 1 inch.

   c Write the ratio 1 cm : 1 inch in the form $1:n$.

   d Use your answer to part **b** to calculate the number of centimetres equivalent to 85 inches.

   e Use the graph to find the number of inches equivalent to 100 cm.

   f Calculate the number of inches equivalent to 1 cm.

   g Write the ratio 1 inch : 1 cm in the form $1:n$.

   h Use your answer to part **f** to calculate the number of inches equivalent to 175 cm.

7 This graph can be used to convert between litres and pints.

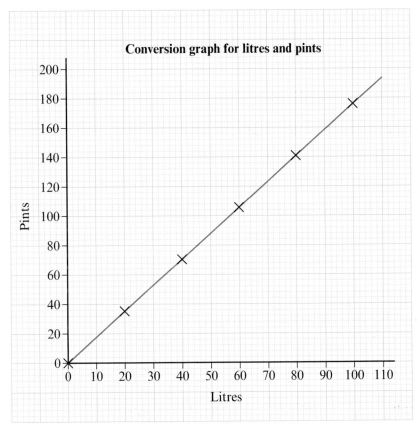

Conversion graph for litres and pints

a Use the graph to find the number of pints equivalent to 100 litres.

b Calculate the number of pints equivalent to 1 litre.

c Write the ratio 1 pint : 1 litre in the form $1 : n$.

d Use your answer to part **b** to calculate the number of pints equivalent to 72 litres.

e Use the graph to find the number of litres equivalent to 100 pints.

f Calculate the number of litres equivalent to 1 pint.

g Write the ratio 1 litre : 1 pint in the form $1 : n$.

h Write the relationship between a capacity in litres, L, and the equivalent capacity in pints, P, as an equation.

i A farmer looked up the average yearly milk yield for a dairy cow in the UK and found it was 11 000 pints.
Convert the average yearly milk yield to litres.

Formulae and expressions

- Simplifying algebraic expressions involving brackets
- Forming algebraic expressions

Keywords

You should know

explanation 1

1 In each algebra caterpillar, the expression in each section is the sum of the expressions in the previous two sections.

What are the missing expressions? Give your answers in their simplest form.

a
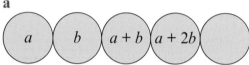

b

c
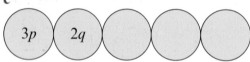

d
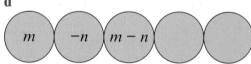

e
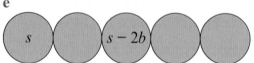

f
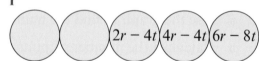

explanation 2

2 In these algebra pyramids, the expression in each brick is the sum of the expressions in the two bricks beneath it.

Copy and complete the pyramids. Give each expression in its simplest form.

a
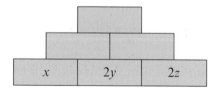

b
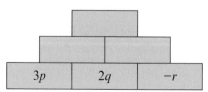

3 Copy and complete these algebra pyramids.
Give each expression in its simplest form.

a

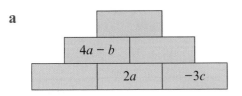

b

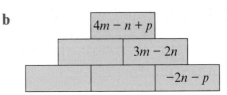

c

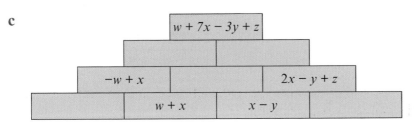

---

explanation 3

---

4 For each function machine, what is the output for each input?
Copy and complete each table. Write your answers in their simplest forms.

a   Input → [× 2] → Output

Input	Output
$x + 2$	
$\dfrac{x}{3}$	
$a - 6$	
$\dfrac{p - 4}{5}$	

b   Input → [× 3] → [− 1] → Output

Input	Output
$a + b$	
$\dfrac{b}{3}$	
$-b + 2$	
$\dfrac{b}{6}$	

159

5 Copy and complete the table to show the output for each input.
Give your answers in their simplest forms.

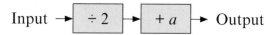

Input → ÷ 2 → + a → Output

Input	Output
$4a + 2b$	
$6 - a$	
$4(x - a)$	
$\dfrac{-4a + 8}{2}$	

6 Write an algebraic expression for the shaded area of each diagram.
Give your answers in their simplest form.

a

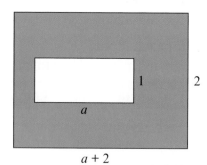

b

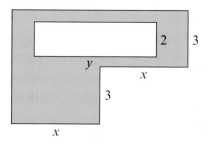

c

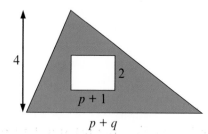

d

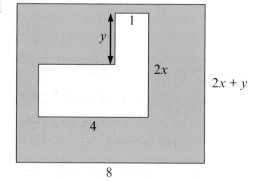

> **Remember**
> Area of a rectangle = length × width
> Area of a triangle = $\frac{1}{2}$ × base × height

Using graphs

- Interpreting distance–time graphs
- Drawing graphs based on real situations
- Giving plausible explanations for the shapes of graphs

Keywords

You should know

explanation 1a   explanation 1b

1 The distance–time graph shows the distance Ben walked at a constant speed.

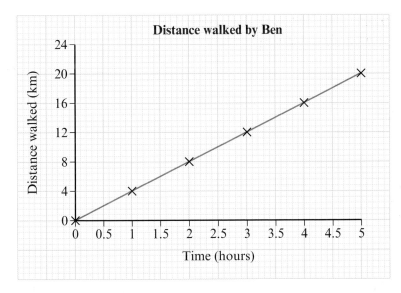

Distance walked by Ben

a How far did Ben walk in 5 hours?

b What was Ben's speed in kilometres per hour?

c Write an equation that links the distance Ben walked (d km) and the time he took (t hours).

d Ben continued to walk at this speed. Use your equation from part **c** to calculate how far Ben walked in 8 hours.

e Ben is going to do a walk for charity. The distance he has to walk is 34 km.

Estimate how long he will take to walk the 34 km.

2 Rebecca was at school and Arjun was at his house 8 km away.
Rebecca started cycling towards Arjun at a steady speed.
At the same time, Arjun started walking in the same direction at a steady speed.
This distance–time graph shows their distances from school.

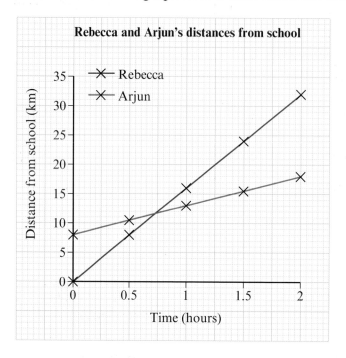

a From the graph, estimate how long it took Rebecca to overtake Arjun.

b Explain how you arrived at your answer to part **a**.

c How far did Rebecca cycle in 2 hours?

d What was Rebecca's speed in kilometres per hour?

e How far did Arjun walk in 2 hours?

f What was Arjun's speed?

g Write an equation that links Rebecca's distance from school (r km) with time (t hours).

h Write an equation that links Arjun's distance from school (a km) with time (t hours).

i When Rebecca overtakes Arjun, they are the same distance from school, so $r = a$. By solving an equation, calculate the time that Rebecca took to overtake Arjun. Give your answer to the nearest minute.

3 Gethin and Abbie were 12 km apart. They started walking at the same time and walked towards each other. Gethin set off from point O. The distance–time graph shows their distances from O.

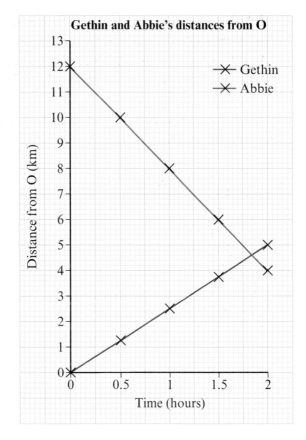

Gethin and Abbie's distances from O

✕ Gethin
✕ Abbie

Distance from O (km)

Time (hours)

a What do straight lines mean on a distance–time graph?

b How far had Gethin travelled after 2 hours?

c What was Gethin's speed?

d Write an equation that links Gethin's distance from O (g km) with time (t hours).

e What was Abbie's speed?

The equation that links Abbie's distance from O (a km) with time (t hours) is $a = 12 - 4t$.

f How far apart were Gethin and Abbie after 1 hour?

g By solving an equation, calculate how long it took Gethin and Abbie to pass each other. Give your answer to the nearest minute.

4 A plumber charges a £50 call out fee and then £25 for each hour worked. The table shows the cost of hiring the plumber for different lengths of time.

Number of Hours	0	1	2	3	4
Cost (£)	50	75	100	125	150

a Plot a graph showing the cost (£C) of hiring the plumber against time (t hours).

b Write an equation that links the cost (£C) and the time (t hours).

c Use your equation to work out how much the plumber would charge for a job lasting 1 hour 45 minutes.

d How long would the plumber have worked if he charged £280 for a job?

5 Two removal companies give a family a quote for helping them move house.

Company A charges a fee of £100 and then £1.50 for each kilometre travelled.

Company B charges a fee of £150 and then £1.30 for each kilometre travelled.

a Copy and complete this table of removal costs.

Distance (km)	0	25	50	100	200	500
Charge Company A (£)	100.00					
Charge Company B (£)	150.00					

b On the same axes, plot a line graph showing the charges for each company.

c From your graph, estimate the distance for which both companies charge the same amount.

d Write an equation that links the charge (£A) and the distance (d km) for Company A.

e Write an equation that links the charge (£B) and the distance (d km) for Company B.

f Calculate the actual distance for which both companies charge the same amount. Use your equations from parts **d** and **e**.

explanation 2

6 This graph shows how the speed of a ball changes with time.

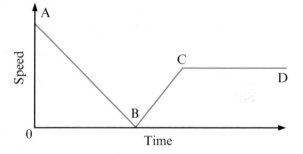

Edna says that the ball is dropped at point A. It hits the ground, then bounces back up and is caught by someone who is standing still.

Ahmed says that the ball is thrown up in the air at point A. It reaches a maximum height, then falls back towards the ground.
On the way down it is caught by someone running at constant speed.

a Which story could be correct? Explain how you know.

b Describe what is happening to the ball between

    i A and B   **ii** B and C   **iii** C and D

Scale drawing

- Converting between lengths on scale drawings and in real life, given the scale
- Drawing diagrams to scale
- Interpreting diagrams drawn to scale

Keywords

You should know

explanation 1a   explanation 1b   explanation 1c

1 Boris draws a plan of his flat to a scale of $1:40$.
Calculate the actual size in metres of the flat.

   a Length of lounge: 12 cm   **b** Width of bedroom: 7.5 cm

   c Length of bathroom: 5.25 cm   **d** Depth of storage cupboard: 1 cm

2 In these questions, the plan lengths and the scale are given.
Calculate the actual lengths. Give your answers in metres.

   a 5 cm, $1:50$ **b** 11 mm, $1:250$ **c** 2 cm, $1:10\,000$

   d 8.5 cm, $1:500$ **e** 2 cm, $1:75$ **f** 1 mm, $1:150\,000$

3 In these questions, the actual lengths and the scale are given.
Calculate the scaled lengths. Give your answers in centimetres.

   a 2 m, $50:1$ **b** 50 mm, $4:1$ **c** 120 m, $500:1$

   d 6 km, $50\,000:3$ **e** 85 cm, $5:3$ **f** 7.5 m, $150:2$

4 A swimming pool is rectangular and has a length of 50 m and a width of 25 m.
Draw a scale diagram of the pool. Use a scale of $1:1000$.

5 The diagram shows a giant tennis court.

Draw a scale diagram of the tennis court. Use a scale of $1:600$.

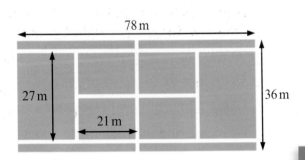

6 The diagram shows a football pitch.

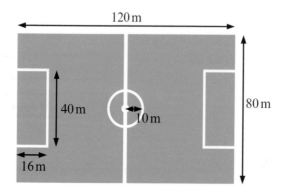

Draw a scale diagram of the football pitch, using a scale of 3:4000.

7 The diagram below shows a rectangular pool 20 m long by 10 m wide.
Rachel stands at R and Steve stands at S.

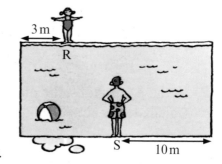

a Draw a scale diagram of the pool, using 1 cm for 2 m.

b Tom swims across the pool. He is always the same distance from Rachel as from Steve. Construct Tom's path across the pool.

> Draw the line segment RS. Every point on the perpendicular bisector of RS is equidistant from R and S.

8 A small rectangular swimming pool WXYZ is 7.5 m long and 5 m wide.

A girl sets off from corner Z and swims towards the edge WX in such a way that she bisects the angle WZY.

On arrival at the edge WX she turns and heads directly towards the corner Y.

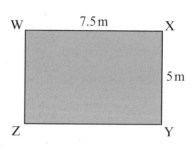

a Using a scale of 1:125, draw a scale diagram of the pool.

b Using a pair of compasses and a ruler, construct the path taken by the girl.

c By measuring the path taken, calculate the actual distance swum by the girl.

Constructions (2)

- Constructing a triangle given the lengths of all three sides
- Constructing a shape made of triangles

Keywords

You should know

explanation 1a   explanation 1b   explanation 1c   explanation 1d

1 Construct each of these triangles.
Use a ruler and a pair of compasses. Do not use a protractor.

a **i** Triangle PQR
PQ = 6 cm, PR = 6 cm, QR = 6 cm

ii What type of triangle is PQR?

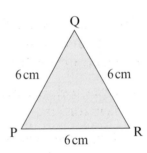

b **i** Triangle XYZ
XY = 4 cm, XZ = 6 cm, YZ = 6 cm

ii What type of triangle is XYZ?

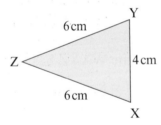

c **i** Triangle ABC
AB = 10 cm, AC = 5 cm, BC = 12 cm

ii What type of triangle is ABC?

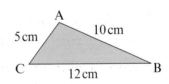

2 Use a ruler and a pair of compasses only for this question.

a Try to construct triangle LMN where LM = 10 cm, LN = 4 cm and MN = 3 cm.

b Is it possible to construct triangle LMN? Give a reason for your answer.

3 The table shows the side lengths of some triangles. Which triangles can be constructed?

Triangle	Dimensions
ABC	AB = 15 cm, AC = 9 cm, BC = 9 cm
DEF	DE = 10 cm, DF = 10 cm, EF = 10 cm
GHI	GH = 20 cm, GI = 9 cm, HI = 7 cm
JKL	JK = 7 cm, JL = 6 cm, KL = 15 cm
MNO	MN = 10 cm, MO = 4 cm, NO = 10 cm

explanation 2a   explanation 2b   explanation 2c

4 Quadrilateral ABCD has these dimensions.

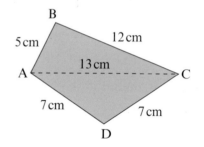

AC = 13 cm   AD = 7 cm

AB = 5 cm   CD = 7 cm

CB = 12 cm

a Using a ruler, draw the line AC.

b Using a pair of compasses, construct the quadrilateral ABCD.

c Measure BD.

5 A kite WXYZ has these dimensions.

WY = 8 cm

WX = 4 cm

YX = 5 cm

a Using a ruler, draw the line WY.

b Using a pair of compasses, construct kite WXYZ.

c Measure XY.

6 A parallelogram DEFG has these dimensions.

DF = 10 cm   DE = 3 cm   DG = 8 cm

a Using a ruler, draw the diagonal DF.

b Using a pair of compasses, construct parallelogram DEFG.

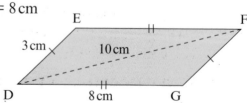

7 The diagram shows a triangular timber roof frame.

Using a ruler and a pair of compasses, construct a diagram of the frame.
Use a scale of $1:200$.

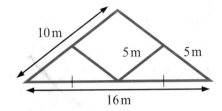

8 The diagram shows a garden EFGH.
EG = 10 m and FH = 7 m

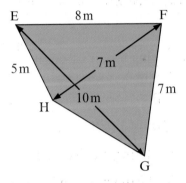

a Using a ruler and a pair of compasses,
construct a diagram of the garden.
Use a scale of $1:125$.

Begin by constructing the triangle EFG.

b Measure the length GH on your diagram.

c What is the length GH in the real garden?

9 A garden designer has drawn a patio in the
shape of a regular hexagon.

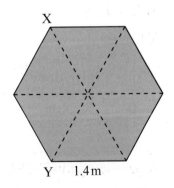

a Using a ruler and a pair of compasses,
construct a scale drawing of the patio.
Use a scale of $1:35$.

Remember that a hexagon is made up of six equilateral triangles

b What is the distance XY on the real patio?

Loci

- Constructing the locus of points from a fixed point
- Constructing the locus of points from a line
- Knowing when to use solid or dashed lines in locus diagrams
- Constructing the locus of points equidistant from a pair of fixed points or lines

Keywords

You should know

explanation 1a explanation 1b

1   Using a pair of compasses, construct the locus of all the points 5 cm from a point X.

2   Using a pair of compasses, construct the locus of all the points no more than 3 cm from a point O.

3   Construct the locus of all the points at least 2 cm, but less than 5 cm, from a point A. Use a pair of compasses.

4   Using a ruler, draw a rectangle ABCD so that AB = 4 cm and AD = 7 cm as shown.

   Shade the locus of all the points in the rectangle that are at least 3 cm from A and C.

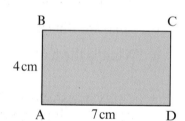

5   Using a ruler, draw a rectangle PQRS, so that PQ = 3 cm and QR = 8 cm.

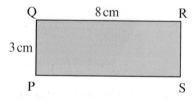

   a   Mark the midpoint of PS. Label it X.

   b   Shade the locus of all the points in the rectangle that are more than 2 cm from X and at least 1 cm from both Q and R.

6 You need a pair of compasses and a ruler for this question.

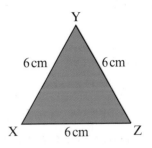

Y

6 cm   6 cm

X   6 cm   Z

a Construct an equilateral triangle XYZ of side length 6 cm as shown.

b Shade the region within the triangle that is at least 3 cm from X, Y and Z.

___

explanation 2

___

7 Copy the diagram onto squared paper. Construct the locus of all the points equidistant from P and Q.

P

Q

8 Copy the diagram onto squared paper. Shade the locus of all the points closer to L than M.

M

L

9 The diagram shows triangle ABC.

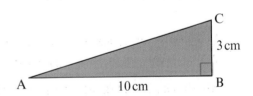

C

3 cm

A   10 cm   B

a Copy the diagram. Construct the locus of points equidistant from A and B.

b On the same diagram, construct the locus of points equidistant from A and C.

c What do you notice about the point where both loci intersect?

10 Mark a point O.

a Draw the locus of points 4 cm from O.

b Mark a point A on this locus.

c Construct part of a locus of points 4 cm from A, such that it intersects with the original locus. Label the point of intersection B.

d Using a ruler, draw the lines OA, AB and OB.

e Describe the shape drawn.

explanation 3

11 Lines OA and OB are both 7 cm and form an angle of 60° as shown.

Copy the diagram and construct the locus of points equidistant from OA and OB.

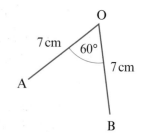

12 A rectangle ABCD has dimensions as shown.

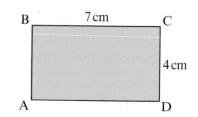

a   Using a ruler, copy the diagram.

b   Construct the locus of points that are equidistant from edges BA and BC. Mark the point of intersection of the locus with side AD as X.

c   Measure the distance XD.

d   Construct the locus of points equidistant from BX and BC.

e   Mark the point of intersection of this locus with the edge of the rectangle Y.

f   Measure the distance YD.

13 A goat is tethered to a post by a rope 9 m long. Draw a diagram of the locus of points in the field that the goat can reach. Use a scale of 1 : 180.

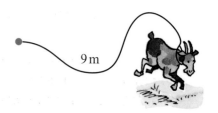

14 A metal rail 4 m long is fixed to a long wall as shown. A horse is tethered to the rail by a rope 2 m long. The rope can run freely along the full length of the rail.

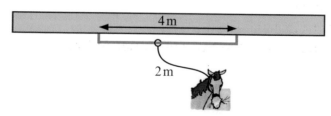

Using a scale of 1 : 50, draw a diagram showing the locus of points that the horse can reach.

15 The diagram shows a courtyard.

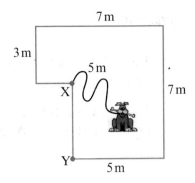

    a A dog is tethered to a hook at corner X by a chain 5 m long.

       Using a scale of 1 : 80, draw a scale diagram. Shade the locus of all the points that the dog can reach.

    b Using a scale of 1 : 80, draw another scale diagram. Shade the locus of all the points that the dog can reach when it is tethered to the hook at corner Y by the same chain.

16 The diagram shows a bare rectangular garden ABCD.
The owner wishes to plant grass in the garden according to these rules.

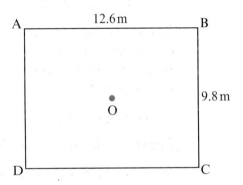

    • It must be further than 2.8 m from the tree planted in the centre of the garden at O.

    • It must be at least 2.1 m from the edge of the garden.

    a Draw a scale diagram of the garden. Use a scale of 1 : 140.

    b Shade the locus of all the points where the grass can be planted.

17 The diagram shows part of a garden.
The line AB represents a tall wall, 6 m long.
Point O lies on the perpendicular bisector of AB.
The shortest distance from O to the wall is 4 m.

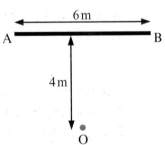

    a Construct the diagram accurately. Use a scale of 1 : 200.

    b A snail is placed at point O.
At top speed, it can travel 8 m in an hour.
Shade the locus of all the points the snail could reach in 1 hour.

Bearings

- Measuring three-figure bearings
- Drawing diagrams involving three-figure bearings

Keywords

You should know

explanation 1a   explanation 1b

1 Calculate the three-figure bearing of B from A in each of these diagrams.

a
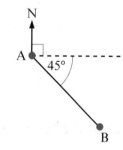

b
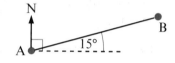

c
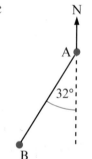

d
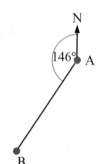

2 Without measuring, calculate the three-figure bearings of A from B in each of the diagrams in question **1** above.

From now on, you will need a protractor. Take North to be vertically up the page.

3 a Copy the diagram on squared paper.

   b Showing your construction clearly, measure the bearing of B from A.

   c Calculate the bearing of A from B.
     Show your working.

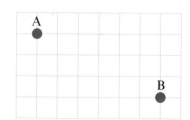

4 a Copy the diagram on squared paper.

b Showing your construction clearly, measure the bearing of Q from P.

c Calculate the bearing of P from Q. Show your working.

d Check your answer to part **c** by measuring.

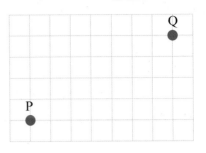

5 a Plot points L and M such that they are 7 cm apart and the bearing of M from L is 020°.

b Calculate the bearing of L from M. Show your working.

c Check your answer to part **b** by measuring.

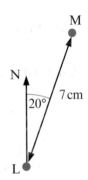

6 a Plot two points J and K, such that they are 3 cm apart and the bearing of K from J is 322°.

b Calculate the bearing of J from K. Show your working.

c Check your answer to part **b** by measuring.

7 Two points K and L are 6 cm apart. L is due north of K. A third point M is on a bearing of 045° from L and on a bearing of 022° from K.

a Plot the points K, L and M.

b To the nearest millimetre, measure the lengths KM and LM.

c Without measuring, calculate the angle LMK. Show your working.

d Calculate the bearing of L from M.

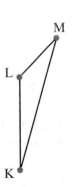

8 Two points X and Y are 8 cm apart on the same horizontal line.
A third point Z is on a bearing of 155° from X and on a bearing of 225° from Y.

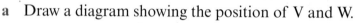

X   Y
                8 cm

a Copy the diagram and locate the position of Z.

b To the nearest millimetre, measure the distance of Z from both X and Y.

c Without measuring, calculate the angle YXZ.

d Without measuring, calculate the angle XZY.

9 Points V and W are 6 cm apart.
The bearing of W from V is 120°.

a Draw a diagram showing the position of V and W.

b Construct the locus of points that are
equidistant from V and W.

c A point U is 4.5 cm from both V and W.
Mark on your diagram the possible positions for point U.

d Measure the bearing of V from each of the possible positions for U.

e Measure the bearing of W from each of the possible positions for U.

10 Town B is 6.50 km due east of town A.
Town C is 4.55 km from A and on a bearing of 125°.

a Using a scale of 1 : 130 000, draw a scale diagram showing the positions of
the three towns relative to each other.

b Measure the bearing of town B from town C.

c Measure the distance in centimetres between B and C on your diagram.

d Calculate the actual distance in kilometres between towns B and C.

11 Ahmed, Brian and Carlos are standing in a large field. Carlos is 210 m due
north of Brian. Ahmed is 135 m and on a bearing of 300° from Brian.

a Using a scale of 1 : 3000, draw a scale diagram showing the position of the
three boys relative to each other.

b What is the bearing of Carlos from Ahmed?

c What is the actual distance between Ahmed and Carlos?

12 Lighthouse L is 32.5 km due west of lighthouse M as shown in the diagram.

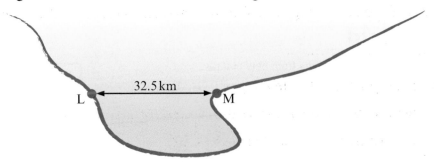

A distress signal is received from a boat B, out at sea. From L the distress signal is on a bearing of 010°. From M the distress signal is on a bearing 315°.

a Using a scale of 1 : 500 000, draw a scale diagram showing the position of L and M relative to each other.

b Using a protractor, find the position of the boat B.

c On your diagram measure the distance of the boat from each of the lighthouses, in centimetres.

d Calculate the actual distance, in kilometres, of the boat from each of the lighthouses.

13 Two observers, P and Q, are standing on a shoreline 9 km apart. The bearing of P from Q is 320°.

Boat X is 8.25 km due east of P.

Boat Y is 4.80 km on a bearing of 025° from Q.

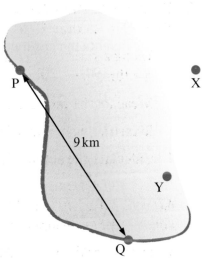

a Using a scale of 1 : 150 000, draw a scale diagram of the positions of P, Q, X and Y relative to each other.

b Measure the distance XY on your diagram.

c Calculate the actual distance between boats X and Y.

d What is the bearing of X from Y?

e What is the bearing and actual distance of X from Q?

f What is the bearing and actual distance of Y from P?

Collecting data

- Preparing grouped frequency tables from lists of data
- Selecting an appropriate class interval for grouping continuous data

Keywords

You should know

explanation 1a explanation 1b

1 Copy and complete the grouped frequency table for each set of data.

a The masses in kilograms of 20 pupils.

| 56 | 71 | 51 | 62 | 62 | 49 | 59 | 56 | 62 | 73 |
| 38 | 55 | 54 | 67 | 69 | 43 | 51 | 61 | 66 | 59 |

Mass (kg)	Frequency
$30 \leq M < 40$	
$40 \leq M < 50$	
$50 \leq M < 60$	
$60 \leq M < 70$	
$70 \leq M < 80$	

b The heights in centimetres of a random sample of 30 sunflowers in a field.

182	194	201	181	199	163	102	192	198	173
152	187	178	122	219	196	190	209	147	172
155	181	186	214	192	116	204	159	188	131

Height (cm)	Frequency
$100 \leq H < 120$	
$120 \leq H < 140$	
$140 \leq H < 160$	
$160 \leq H < 180$	
$180 \leq H < 200$	
$200 \leq H < 220$	

2 Copy and complete the grouped frequency table for each set of data.

   a The time in seconds taken by 20 sprinters to run 200 m.

      22.47   22.71   23.01   23.96   21.03   22.68   22.93   22.55   24.00   23.21

      23.84   25.77   24.10   22.89   23.12   23.45   22.88   22.61   21.66   23.57

Time (s)	Frequency
$21 \le T < 22$	
$22 \le T < 23$	
$23 \le T < 24$	
$24 \le T < 25$	
$25 \le T < 26$	

   b The mass in grams of the marmalade in a sample of twenty 100 g jars of marmalade.

100.38	100.49	100.26	99.82	99.67
100.44	100.36	101.09	100.25	100.39
100.22	99.51	99.82	99.41	100.33
99.56	100.05	100.49	101.27	99.62

Mass (g)	Frequency
$99.0 \le M < 99.5$	
$99.5 \le M < 100.0$	
$100.0 \le M < 100.5$	
$100.5 \le M < 101.0$	
$101.0 \le M < 101.5$	

3 The table shows the distance in kilometres of 20 major cities from London.

City	Distance from London (km)	City	Distance from London (km)
New York	5569	Cape Town	9670
Moscow	2500	New Delhi	6711
Beijing	8137	Riyadh	4951
Sydney	16 993	Helsinki	1821
Lisbon	1585	Warsaw	1447
Paris	342	Havana	7491
Barcelona	1139	Los Angeles	8755
Rome	1433	Ottawa	5360
Rio de Janeiro	9278	Buenos Aires	11 140
Cairo	3511	Wellington	18 815

a Construct an appropriate grouped frequency table for the distances in the table.

b Give a reason for your choice of class interval.

Analysing data (2)

- Estimating the mean of grouped continuous data
- Identifying the modal class of grouped data
- Realising that the mean of grouped data is often very close to the mean of the raw data

Keywords

You should know

explanation 1a   explanation 1b

1 a These are the playing times in minutes of tracks on two of Finn's CDs.

| 4.17 | 2.78 | 1.63 | 4.02 | 16.52 | 4.67 | 2.05 | 4.67 | 5.33 | 6.50 |
| 5.97 | 9.78 | 8.77 | 17.55 | 6.80 | 4.12 | 6.90 | 3.72 | 5.25 | 7.85 |

Find the following times in minutes and seconds.

  i The mean playing time   **ii** The median playing time

  iii The range of the playing time   **iv** The modal playing time

b Finn decides to group the data and constructs this grouped frequency table.

Time (mins)	Frequency
$0.00 \le T < 4.00$	
$4.00 \le T < 8.00$	
$8.00 \le T < 12.00$	
$12.00 \le T < 16.00$	
$16.00 \le T < 20.00$	

$0.00 \le T < 4.00$ represents times from 0 minutes up to, but not including 4 minutes.

Copy and complete the grouped frequency table.

c Finn then gives the grouped frequency data to a friend, who decides to analyse the grouped data.

Use the grouped data to find these times in minutes and seconds.

  i The estimated mean playing time

  ii The modal group

d Comment on any similarities and/or differences in the results from parts **a** and **c**.

2 The grouped frequency diagram, shows the lengths of 20 snakes at a snake farm.

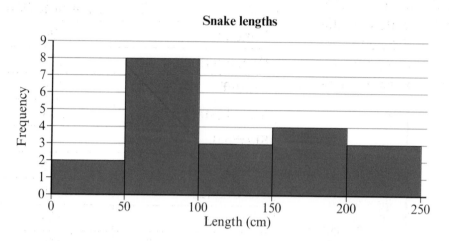

Snake lengths

a What is the mid-interval value of the group $50 \leq L < 100$?

b Copy and complete this grouped frequency table. Add extra rows for the intervals $150 \leq L < 200$ and $200 \leq L < 250$.

Length (cm)	Mid-interval value	Frequency
$0 \leq L < 50$		
$50 \leq L < 100$		
$100 \leq L < 150$		

c What is the modal group?

d Estimate the mean length of the snakes at the farm.

3 Isabel had a project to research the average playing time of films at her local cinema. Over a 4-week period she recorded the duration of all the films that the cinema played. These are the times in minutes.

138 131 158 125 117 114 140 118 94

138 121 91 120 115 129 105 125 149

a Calculate the following times in minutes and seconds.

i the mean duration **ii** the median duration

iii the modal duration **iv** the range of the film durations

b Isabel then decides to group her data. Using a class interval of 10 minutes, construct and complete an appropriate grouped frequency table.

c Use the grouped data to find these times in minutes and seconds.

i The estimated mean duration **ii** The modal group

4 Ryan lives in Cambridge. One summer he decides to visit 15 of his friends in different cities around the UK. The cities and their distances by road from Cambridge are given in the table.

City	Distance from Cambridge (km)
London	98
Portsmouth	216
Cardiff	326
Manchester	258
Sheffield	197
Glasgow	566
Nottingham	139
Liverpool	309
Newcastle-upon-Tyne	369
Edinburgh	536
Exeter	401
Perth	599
Birmingham	155
Leeds	237
Blackpool	366

a Use this data to find the following distances.

   i The mean distance from Cambridge

   ii The median distance from Cambridge

   iii The modal distance from Cambridge

   iv The range of the distances

b Construct an appropriate grouped frequency table for this data.

c Use your grouped data to find these distances.

   i The estimated mean distance from Cambridge

   ii The modal group

d Comment on any similarities and/or differences in your answers to parts **a** and **c**.

Comparing distributions

- Interpreting more complex graphs
- Giving possible reasons for the shapes of graphs
- Justifying explanations using the evidence from calculations

Keywords

You should know

explanation 1a explanation 1b

1 Two types of battery were tested to compare how long they last. 30 batteries of each type were tested under the same conditions. The results are shown in the tables.

Battery A	
Duration (hours)	**Frequency**
$0 \leq t < 5$	2
$5 \leq t < 10$	4
$10 \leq t < 15$	5
$15 \leq t < 20$	6
$20 \leq t < 25$	4
$25 \leq t < 30$	5
$30 \leq t < 35$	4

Battery B	
Duration (hours)	**Frequency**
$0 \leq t < 5$	0
$5 \leq t < 10$	0
$10 \leq t < 15$	12
$15 \leq t < 20$	13
$20 \leq t < 25$	4
$25 \leq t < 30$	1
$30 \leq t < 35$	0

$0 \leq t < 5$ means the duration includes 0 and goes up to 5 but does *not* include 5.

a Draw a grouped frequency diagram for the results of each battery.

b Calculate an estimate for the mean duration of each battery.

c Which battery is more reliable? Justify your answer.

d A youth group is doing a sponsored 24-hour dance. They need to choose the batteries that are most likely to last the full 24 hours. Which battery type should they choose? Justify your answer.

2 The age distribution of the population in two countries is shown below.
The distribution is given as a percentage for each age group.

Country A	
Age (years)	**Percentage**
$0 \leq A < 20$	24
$20 \leq A < 40$	30
$40 \leq A < 60$	28
$60 \leq A < 80$	14
$80 \leq A < 100$	4

Country B	
Age (years)	**Percentage**
$0 \leq A < 20$	40
$20 \leq A < 40$	28
$40 \leq A < 60$	19
$60 \leq A < 80$	10
$80 \leq A < 100$	3

a Draw a grouped frequency diagram for each country.

b Calculate an estimate for the mean age of the population of country A.

c Calculate an estimate for the mean age of the population of country B.

d Describe in your own words the difference in the age distributions between the two countries.

e One of the countries is from the developed world and one is from the developing world. Which country is likely to be from the developing world?

f Justify your answer to part **e**.

3 The table shows the temperature at noon in two holiday resorts, A and B, every other day during the month of August. One resort is in England, the other is in Portugal.

Day	1	3	5	7	9	11	13	15	17	19	21	23	25	27	29	31
Noon temperature (°C) Resort A	32	31	28	34	29	27	31	30	35	31	31	27	32	31	36	30
Noon temperature (°C) Resort B	24	24	31	24	21	22	26	25	32	25	25	24	26	28	19	19

a   On the same axes draw line graphs to show the temperatures at noon in both resorts during August.

b   For each resort calculate these statistics.

  i   the mean daily midday temperature

  ii   the median daily midday temperature

  iii   the modal midday temperature

  iv   the range in the monthly temperatures

c   By referring to the line graphs and your calculations in part b, state which of the resorts is likely to be the one in England.

4 This graph shows the mean house price in different countries of the UK from 1999 to 2007.

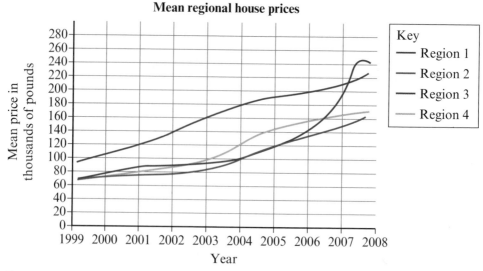

Comment on any similarities and differences in mean house prices in the four regions since 1999.